From Berlin to Jerusalem

Gershom Scholem in Sils-Maria, Switzerland, 1976

Gershom Scholem

From Berlin to Jerusalem

MEMORIES OF MY YOUTH

*Translated from the German
by Harry Zohn*

SCHOCKEN BOOKS · NEW YORK

First published by Schocken Books 1980
10 9 8 7 6 5 4 3 2 1   80 81 82 83

English translation copyright © 1980 by Schocken Books Inc.
Originally published in German as *Von Berlin nach Jerusalem*
by Suhrkamp Verlag © Suhrkamp Verlag Frankfurt am Main 1977

Library of Congress Cataloging in Publication Data
Scholem, Gershom Gerhard, 1897–
    From Berlin to Jerusalem.

    Translation of Von Berlin nach Jerusalem.
    1. Scholem, Gershom Gerhard, 1897–   2.Scholars,
Jewish—Germany—Biography.   3. Scholars, Jewish—
Israel—Biography.   4. Jews in Germany—Intellectual
life.   I. Title
BM755.S295A3413   296.8'3 [B]   79–25678

Manufactured in the United States of America

To the memory of my brother Werner
born in December 1895 in Berlin
murdered in July 1940 in Buchenwald

Also by Gershom Scholem:

Kabbalah
Major Trends in Jewish Mysticism
The Messianic Idea in Judaism
    And Other Essays on Jewish Spirituality
On Jews & Judaism in Crisis
    Selected Essays
On the Kabbalah & Its Symbolism
Sabbatai Sevi
    The Mystical Messiah
Zohar—The Book of Splendor
    Basic Readings from the Kabbalah (Ed.)

Contents

I

Background and Childhood (1897–1910)

IN RECORDING SOME remembrances of my early life—before 1925, the year I was appointed lecturer at the newly founded Hebrew University in Jerusalem—I am naturally aware that there is no dearth of memoirs describing one's youth in Berlin, though I cannot say I've read any of them. But I suppose the outstanding feature in this case would be the fact that I am describing the life of a young Jew whose path took him from the Berlin of his childhood and youth to Jerusalem and Israel. This path appeared to me to be singularly direct and illuminated by clear signposts; to others, including my own family, it often seemed incomprehensible, if not vexatious.

I come from a family of Berlin Jews who lived in Glogau, Lower Silesia ("Greater Glogau") until the second decade of the nineteenth century, when some of its members migrated to Berlin. The name Scholem is extremely rare as a family name, but was quite common as a first name among Ashkenazic Jews; it constitutes the Ashkenazic pronunciation of the Hebrew word for peace, *shalom.* In

1

my lifetime I have encountered only two other families named Scholem, and neither one was related to us; one was from Upper Silesia, and the other was from Neustadt near Kaiserslautern and other places in the Palatinate. The poet Guillaume Apollinaire served the latter family as a tutor for some time. In accordance with the Prussian edict of 1812 concerning the Jews, all Jews were obliged, among other things, to adopt permanent family names, for the constant change of names had prevented the authorities from keeping proper records. According to family legend, my great-great-grandfather was summoned to the town hall and asked what his name was. He did not understand the question and answered "Scholem," whereupon the official entered it as his family name. When he was asked his first name, he impatiently repeated "Scholem." This is how we received our family name. In other documents I found my great-great-grandfather mentioned as Scholem Elias—that is, Scholem, son of Elias. The truth of the matter is that he died between 1809 and 1811; thereupon his widow Zipporah appeared at the town hall and declared that she was adopting her late husband's name as her own and her children's family name.

When I was a child, an oil painting of Zipporah—my grandfather's grandmother—hung in our parlor; it had been painted in 1821 or 1831 and demonstrated a clear family resemblance to the Scholems I knew. It was said that this portrait (which still hangs in the home of my oldest brother in Sidney) had been painted by a relative in Glogau who had participated in the Wars of Liberation. It shows my great-great-grandmother enthroned like a true Jewish matriarch. In the "Berlin Room," as the large central room used for dining was called in the middle-class apartments of the time, there hung photographs of my grandparents and great-grandparents, and next to these was a group picture showing my mother with her girl friends; it bore an inscription that has an odd ring to it today: "Israelitischer Jungfrauenverein [Association of Israelite Maidens] Charlottenburg 1888." In those days no one smiled at such an inscription. Most of these young ladies constituted my mother's circle of friends in later years. When the last maiden got married in the early 1890s, the association came to a natural end.

When I was born toward the end of 1897—by the Friedrichsgracht in Old Berlin, somewhat east of the Spittelmarkt, where today there is only a park with shrubs and benches in place of the bombed houses—my family had been residing in Berlin for three generations, my great-grandfather (who died in 1845) having moved there shortly after the Wars of Liberation.

My family had progressed from the traditional Orthodox Jewish lifestyle of the Jews from Silesia and Poznań, who constituted the overwhelming majority of Berlin Jewry, to an extensive assimilation of the lifestyle of their surroundings. In the eighteenth century, Glogau was the largest Jewish community in Silesia, and my other paternal ancestors had come from small towns like Beuthen an der Oder, Auras, and Köben. This is not surprising, for in general no Jews were allowed to live in Breslau until the abovementioned Jewish edict of 1812, which gave the Jews from those provinces that had belonged to Prussia before the partitions of Poland certain civil rights, particularly the economically all-important right of free movement. The only Jews excepted from this prohibition were the possessors of a so-called general privilege from the King of Prussia, and that meant a few rich families (and their rather numerous "servant staff") that had participated in Frederick the Great's mercantilist policies with especial vigor and success—an initiative which the Prussian authorities appreciated and supported. The great majority of Jews lived in the country and in small towns

from where a considerable number of the next generation flocked to Breslau and Berlin.

My mother's ancestors, the Hirsches and Pflaums, came
from Reetz, a small place in the northeasternmost corner
of the "Neumark," and from the large Jewish communities Rawicz and Lissa [Leszno] in the province of Poznań.
My mother, however, never spoke of the province of
Poznań, but always of the "Grand Duchy," as a living tes-
timonial to the special regulations that during her parents'
youth, until 1847–48, had governed the Jews from the
"Grand Duchy of Warsaw" formed under Napoleon—
that is, those Jews who lived in the parts that had been
returned to Prussia by the Congress of Vienna. That
was also the background of all the families with which
my parents or their relatives associated or into which
they married.

After the early death of her husband, my father's
grandmother—Esther Holländer, who had begun to call
herself Ernestine Scholem—owned a Jewish restaurant
(the kind that was then called a kosher *Garküche,* an
inexpensive eating place) in Old Berlin's Klosterstrasse,
not far from the Gymnasium zum Grauen Kloster. When
my father spoke of such things, he would tell us that his
brothers' various fathers-in-law had all eaten at his grandmother's place as young fellows upon their arrival from
Poznań and Silesia. In this way the families had become
acquainted and a close friendship with my mother's parents had been formed. When I was a child, my father once
took us to the house where Grandmother had lived and
cooked. There was no vestige of any such kosher kitchen
in our house. In the milieu in which I grew up, only an old
uncle (by marriage) of my father's still ran a strictly kosher
household with his three unmarried daughters until his
death. I remember pumping him for information about
our ancestors in 1910, on his eightieth birthday.

For three generations, from 1861 to 1938, my paternal family owned first one and then two printshops in Berlin. I still have the work that my grandfather had to set in type to qualify as a journeyman in 1858 after years of training as an apprentice and assistant in various print-shops: the *Poetische Schriften* [Poetic Writings] of Friedrich Heimbertsohn Hinze, a completely forgotten writer from the same town as Thomas Mann. The work was published in 1859.

My uncle also owned a Jewish prayerbook set in type by my grandfather. Born in Berlin in 1833 and given a strictly Jewish education in his parental home and in the orphanage of the Jewish Community Council, my grandfather personified the transition of the Jews to German culture. In accordance with a widespread Jewish custom, he was named after his deceased grandfather, that is, Scholem Scholem. The official, however, refused to enter his first name on the birth certificate (I still have the original in my possesion), and after considerable debate they agreed on what might be termed a Germanized form of the name: Solm. No one ever used it. When my grandfather became an enthusiatic Wagnerian in the 1850s, he henceforth called himself Siegfried Scholem, and it was under this name that his printshop was entered in the trade register. On his gravestone, which may still be seen at the Jewish cemetery at Weissensee in East Berlin, the Hebrew inscription still refers to him as Scholem Scholem, but the German inscription on the front reads Siegfried. The gravestone of my father (1925) bore no Hebrew inscription.

My father, Arthur, who was born in Berlin in 1863, had also had a long period as an apprentice and journeyman in a major printshop there. In the early 1880s he had also worked as a typesetter in London for a year while living with an uncle. One branch of the family had emigrated to London around 1860, and up to the time of my childhood there were contacts with those relatives, some of whom emigrated to Brooklyn, where I came across them in 1938. In 1883 young Scholem returned with a flowing full beard, but later this gave way to a moustache twirled upward in the Wilhelminian manner. Until the outbreak of World War I he would go to a café by the Gertraudtenbrücke every Sunday where for two hours he read the *Manchester Guardian,* a paper that shaped his views at least as much as the *Berliner Tageblatt* (to which we subscribed). After his return from England he joined his father's firm and did his best to expand it. My father and my grandfather both had quick tempers, but were otherwise quite different and did not get along with each other very well. In 1892, two years after his marriage, my father went into business for himself; at first his firm was small and struggled with considerable difficulties. Soon after his fortieth birthday he developed heart trouble and went to Bad Nauheim every summer to take an extended course of treatment. In his absence my mother, who had done the bookkeeping all along and also held power of attorney, ran the business. During the years when I was growing up we had to be considerate of Father's bad heart and were told to spare him excitement as much as possible. For this reason our relationship with him was not a particularly close one, and my father sought satisfaction in his activities in professional organizations and the health insurance plan of the graphic trades; for more than twenty-five years he devoted a great deal of his free time to the latter. He was a short and stocky man, nearsighted and completely bald by the age of forty, a trait that we all inherited from him.

My mother, too, was not very tall, so my own height of close to six feet must go back to the Hirsch side of the family. She also was a native of Berlin, but she had spent several of her childhood years in small towns like Seesen, not far from the Harz mountains, and Leobschütz, Silesia, where her father had worked as a housefather in two Jewish institutions, one of them an orphanage. Later he returned to Berlin with his family and resumed his commercial career. He still had lively Jewish interests, and in the 1880s or 1890s he became the cofounder of a small Reform synagogue on the Schulstrasse in Charlottenburg, the district of Berlin in which he lived. My grandfathers died when I was only three and six respectively, so I barely have a physiognomic memory of them. On the other hand, until I was ten or eleven I had to visit my grandmothers every other week, so I still have a clear memory of these two ladies, who struck me at the time as positively ancient. Grandmother Amalie Scholem, who lived not far from us, was regarded as a vigorous and resolute woman. Even when her very good-looking but weak husband was still alive, she was the absolute mistress of the house and the business. To the last she was an extremely thrifty woman. Before every visit to her we were expressly enjoined not to accept any sweets or fruits that she might offer us, since she was in the habit of keeping the food that her four sons brought her when they came visiting until it became moldy. Because I developed a sweet tooth early on, I still vividly remember my disappointment in the face of those half-moldy chocolate creams. At any rate, I was consoled by the fact that she always handed me five or ten pfennigs when I left, which sum I promptly took to the candy store across the street, and fittingly invested in an ice cream sandwich or chocolate cookies with poppy seeds. My mother repeatedly told me that her mother-in-law had expected her, above all else, to provide a granddaughter to be named Philippine, after her late mother. When, at the birth of the fourth grandson, I too dashed this hope shamefully, her mother-in-law was so indignant, according to my mother, that she did not speak with her for several months. In her room, and afterwards in Uncle Theobald's, there was a wonderful big grandfather clock with a pendulum, made in 1810 by her father David Schlesinger as his journeyman's project in a clockmaker's shop. The clock struck every quarter hour and was greatly prized. It is still ticking today in the home of my cousin Dinah at Tiv'on, near Haifa.

All my grandparents had numerous brothers and sisters, many of whom also lived in Berlin. A maternal uncle of my mother's was court photographer by appointment to Emperor Frederick III and the father of two sons who constituted the wealthiest branch of the family. My mother maintained friendly and sometimes even close relations with these cousins and their sisters, while my father had great reservations about the somewhat ostentatious and pretentious social life of these relatives, and accompanied his wife on her visits only with great reluctance. In my generation there was an uncommonly beautiful cousin named Margot Pflaum, the only such specimen we could boast.

In general, however, our family circle was part of the Jewish middle class and lower middle class, the bourgeoisie which around the middle of the last century had worked its way up from small and very modest beginnings, had not infrequently attained prosperity if not real wealth, and stayed almost entirely within its own socio-economic group. Treitschke's once-notorious scornful remark about the ambitious young pants salesmen from the province of Poznań who had flocked to Berlin applied to those very men whom I knew in their old age as the prosperous owners of factories that produced bathtubs or sausage skins. My aunts by marriage were the daughters of such families. Only in few instances did the transition to

academic professions take place in my parents' generation.
My father's youngest brother was sent to the Gymnasium
and then studied medicine amidst great hardships. But
his other brother, who was passionately interested in
ethnology and the Orient, had to give up his plans and
enter his father's business, in which he achieved considerable prosperity. My mother's two siblings, on the other
hand, were both able to receive a higher education, though
the financial basis was very limited. Her sister became
one of the first female doctors of Berlin, and her brother
became a chemist and patent attorney. The only one of
my father's relatives whose name was universally known
in Berlin and its theatrical history was Felix Holländer,
the dramatic adviser of Max Reinhardt and a novelist
published by S. Fischer. However, for reasons not known
to me this relationship was not particularly cultivated.

In their youth my father and two of his brothers were
very active in the Berlin gymnastics association, probably
the most characteristic organization of the petite bourgeoisie. Until the eighties it was decidedly liberal in
character, but from 1890 on it was increasingly open to
anti-Semitic tendencies. In my parents' bookcase there
was a pamphlet which my father had published in 1887,
Allerlei für Deutschlands Turner [Miscellany for Germany's
Gymnasts]. We were a typical liberal middle-class family
in which assimilation to things German, as people put it at
the time, had progressed quite far. In our home there
were only a few perceptible relics of Judaism, such as the
use of Jewish idiomatic expressions, which my father
avoided and forbade us to use, but which my mother gladly
employed, especially when she wanted to make a point.
If, for example, she wanted to underline the insignificance
of an event, she invariably repeated an expression that
her mother had imported from Rawicz to Berlin: *"Hat
sich die Kose bemeikelt,"* which means "So the goat shits

on itself" (or in other words, "So what else is new?"). One of my uncles, whom the anti-Semitism of the gymnasts had turned into an early Zionist, also used to employ such expressions during family get-togethers with marked provocative intent and to the displeasure of my father. The word *nebbich,* an expression of regret with particularly emotional overtones, became a permanent part of my vocabulary one day when I had to accompany my mother on a visit to her cousin and Aunt Grete Borchard remarked about me: *"Gerhardchen ist nebbich so anständig"* [Jerry is such a decent boy, poor thing]. That wasn't a sentence one forgot easily.

As far as Jewish ritual was concerned, in our home only Friday evening, which was considered family night, and the Seder on the eve of Passover were observed. On these occasions all the Scholems would get together at my grandmother's home, later at the home of my father or that of one or another of his brothers, in turn. The *Kiddush,* the Hebrew blessing for the Sabbath, was still chanted but only half understood. That did not keep people from using the Sabbath candles to light a cigarette or cigar afterwards. Since the prohibition to smoke on the Sabbath was one of the most widely known Jewish regulations, there was deliberate mockery in this act. During Passover week, bread and matzos were next to each other in two breadbaskets, and matzo with honey was very popular with us children. On the most solemn Jewish holiday, Yom Kippur, which was still observed as a fast day by the overwhelming majority, my father went to work and no one thought of fasting. My mother took her mother, who strictly kept the fast, to synagogue, and my uncles' wives, at least, observed the fast day and went to synagogue. Malicious souls used to say in the years before World War I that a headwaiter stood at the entrance to the well-known restaurant next to the Grosse Synagoge on Oranienburger Strasse (corner of Artilleriestrasse) and addressed the guests in their holiday finery as follows: "The gentlemen who are fasting will be served in the back room." On the other hand, once or twice a year my father used to make a speech at the dinner table in praise of the mission of the Jews. According to him, that mission was to proclaim to the world pure monotheism and a purely rational morality. Baptism, he said, was an unprincipled and servile act. Around 1910 the monthly newsletter of the Berlin Jewish Community Council, which was sent to all members free of charge, began to print on the last page the names of those who had left the Jewish fold. (According to the laws then in force, the district court had to notify the Council so that the persons involved would be exempted from paying taxes to it.) This column was widely and carefully read even when nothing else in the whole issue was. I still remember several cases, very famous at the time, in which such publication turned out to be so embarrassing to the people involved that they vainly tried to take legal action to prevent the exposure.

My parents had learned to read Hebrew in their childhood. My mother, who had already forgotten her Hebrew, surprised me one day when I had begun to study the language myself and to attend the synagogue; in response to a remark I had made, probably in a somewhat condescending tone about her Jewish knowledge, she recited from memory—spontaneously and without a single mistake—the complete text of the most important Jewish prayer, *Shema Yisrael,* the Jewish creed which comprises six verses from Deuteronomy. To be sure, she had no idea what the prayer meant. In accordance with Jewish custom, her

father had taught her at the age of four or five to say it as
an evening prayer on going to bed, and almost fifty years
later she was still familiar with it.

In 1906, when I was going on nine, we moved from the
Friedrichsgracht to a larger apartment at Neue Grünstrasse 26, just two or three minutes away. Opposite our
apartment I could see the entrance to the building of the
Kirchengemeinde St. Petri [St. Peter's Parish] which was
located in a rather large garden. While most of the houses
on the street had been bombed, I could still find this
entrance with the old sign in 1946. Next to it stood the
printshop of Otto von Holten with a very elegant facade
and sign—my first and entirely unconscious encounter
with the place where the writings of Stefan George and
the circle around the periodical *Blätter für die Kunst* were
printed. When I became acquainted with George's poems,
some of which have made a profound and lasting impression on me, in 1913 and 1914, I viewed the house across
the street with particular interest. While walking on
Mohrenstrasse one day I found the first public edition of
the volume *Das Jahr der Seele* [The Year of the Soul] in a
window of Gsellius, the well-known dealer in secondhand
books. This volume so attracted me, possibly because of
its title, that I purchased it and thus gained access to
George's poetry. Later I bought several of his other books,
among them—right after its appearance in early 1914—
Der Stern des Bundes [The Star of the Covenant]. When
I reread that book eight years later, it so enraged me—
despite a few wonderful poems—that I tossed the volume
out of my library and gave it to my cousin Heinz Pflaum,
who had deeper sympathy for George and his school.
However, a great deal from *Das Jahr der Seele, Der Teppich
des Lebens* [The Tapestry of Life], and *Der siebente Ring*
[The Seventh Ring] has stuck with me.

In the new apartment, where I spent almost all of my remaining years in Berlin, my brothers and I could of course no longer practice spitting cherry pits into the Spree across the street. But in other respects our move caused no great changes in our environment. My school, the Luisenstädtisches Realgymnasium on Sebastianstrasse, where I was to study Latin four hours a week for nine years, remained the same. I played in the nearby Märkischer Park, where the Märkisches Museum was just being completed, and played marbles there with boys around my age. Across the street, on Inselstrasse, was the storage yard of a lumber or coal company, and on its lattice fence one could usually read chalk graffiti such as *"Gustav ist doof"* [Gus is a dummy] and the like. The Berlin dialect of those districts was still quite uncorrupted, and I liked it all the more because its use at our dinner table was strictly forbidden. Through all the transformations of my life, I have retained the Berlin cadence of my speech.

When I was tired of playing games, I would often walk the short distance from the park to the banks of the Spree opposite the Janowitzbrücke metropolitan railway station. This was where the excursion steamers left for Grünau. But that was not what fascinated me. Rather, I would spend long periods of time staring across the Spree at the long-distance trains that went by the station at relatively low speed, and reading the signboards on the individual cars; even at that distance my eyes were good enough to decipher them. I was fascinated by the strange place names, which I later looked up in Andreä's big family atlas at home. Frequently the destinations were emphasized with larger letters than the interim stops, and thus names like Hoek van Holland, Eydtkuhnen, and Oświęcim (a name that sometimes appeared on express trains) became familiar to me, without my having any idea that behind this foreign-sounding name, the border station between

Upper Silesia and Galicia, was nothing other than Auschwitz. I could not get my fill of those trains and those names which brought me something of the magic of faraway places. I was ten or eleven at the time.

At the age of eleven or twelve my mother took me to the Schillertheater for the first time, and following the custom of Jewish families we saw a play by Schiller. In my case it was *Wilhelm Tell*. I still vividly remember the Schiller festival of 1909 in the Deutsches Theater, where Joseph Kainz recited, or "performed," *"Die Glocke"* [The Song of the Bell] before a full house. My parents had seen to it that all of us attended this festive performance, for they expected it to make a lasting impression upon us. I was not responsive to this performance, however, and in general my attitude toward the theater has remained a highly reserved one. I have frequently read dramas, but I have rarely if ever felt the need to see them performed. My mother, who was very enthusiastic about the theatre, sometimes induced me to go to the Schiller-Theater East on Wallnertheaterstrasse. Two or three times I went to the Thalia Theater, only a few minutes from our home. There I saw Fritzi Massary, whose star was in the ascendant at the time, in an operetta a few years before World War I— the only operetta I went to see in Germany before my emigration. This, to be sure, did not mean that I took no cognizance of the operetta hits of the day. Whether I wanted to or not, I heard them from the phonographs and the bands whenever I went skating in the Botanical Garden on Potsdamer Strasse or in the Ice Palace near the Bayrischer Platz. My memory developed an incredible receptivity for trivia (a faculty which I have unfortunately retained), so I still find myself humming some of those songs, as well as the songs that we had to sing at school while marching in the gym. I am sorry to say that I never managed to find an angel who might have allowed me to exchange these and similar items in my memory bank for other, more desirable ones. Among the many magical formulas that I have studied in the course of my life, I have never put my hands on a formula for this particular feat.

In the theatrical city of Munich, where I spent two and a half years, I attended the theater all of two times. On the other hand, that was where, in 1920, I met Erich Engel, at the time a producer at the Kammerspiele. This meeting, however, I owed not to the theater, for which I had no taste, but to Rosa Okun, a Russian Jew from Hamburg and a close friend of the girl who would become my first wife, Elsa Burchhardt. Engel had passionately fallen in love at first sight with this girl, who radiated an indescribable charm, and he remained close to her for more than twenty years, until her death in the late 1930s. Engel was small and rotund and had pronouncedly Jewish features, though he actually had only one Jewish grandmother, of whom he was very proud. He was passionately interested in everything philosophical, and we had many friendly arguments in those days and in later years when I visited Berlin from Israel. During the Nazi period he was marvelous to Rosa (whom he always called Sonja), but she was already very ill at the time.

A strange phenomenon of Jewish Berlin was the little Herrnfeld Theater, less than five minutes from our home, where the Herrnfeld brothers, two excellent actors (who were baptized Jews), performed Jewish comedies for years before an almost entirely Jewish public—the only audience able to appreciate the idiom and intonation of these plays, which often remained in the repertoire for a very long time. I once went to see one of these stock comedies, *Die Klabriaspartie* [The Card Game], and my father waxed very indignant over it, for he claimed that such plays promoted anti-Semitism—as though anti-Semitism had been waiting for the Herrnfeld brothers.

In those years, especially from 1909 on, I was far more attracted to the movie theater on Kommandantenstrasse, at the end of Neue Grünstrasse. At the time the movie houses were generally known as *Flimmerkisten* [flicker boxes]. One did not go to see a definite program; instead, tickets were sold by numbers that were collected at regular intervals. Thus one would buy numbers 8 to 13, for example—but the films went on endlessly. They featured Asta Nielsen and Max Linder, whom I can picture to this day, in crime films or farces, and the screen flickered so much that one's eyes started to hurt. Everything was designed to produce the greatest possible amount of laughter or horror, and the actors' movements were very comical, possibly because of the primitive shooting techniques then used. (Such techniques are hardly imaginable today.) During the war I rarely went to the movies, if ever, and only when I was living in Berne in 1918 and 1919 did I begin to go more often again in the company of my cousin Lony. At that time the brief sketches by Charlie Chaplin which were shown before the main program were becoming big attractions. If I ask myself what major films I remember from my youth, only the anti-German war film *The Four Horsemen of the Apocalypse* and the expressionistic masterpiece *The Cabinet of Dr. Caligari* come to mind. Even though I did not care for literary expressionism—I liked the poetry more than the prose—I was able to admire the latter film without reservations, and I have gone to see it again a number of times.

While my relationship to my father was characterized from early on by a certain distance, one that only increased over the years, my mother Betty played a much greater role in my youth. It is true that she went to work at nine in the morning, when I was already in school, and came home only for the noonday meal and the rest period that followed it, and then went to the shop for two hours in the afternoon three or four times a week, so that we saw very little of her during the day; still, her presence loomed large. Between 1913 and 1917, when I was the only child in the house, she permitted me to "wrap her in" after the noonday meal (for which the cook was responsible, my mother having that morning given her the three-course menu). To "wrap her in" meant that my mother would stretch out on a very fine chaise longue in her bedroom and I would cover her with a large camel's hair blanket (which is still in my possession today). In return I was permitted to take one or two bars of Swiss chocolate from a drawer and held a ten- or fifteen-minute conversation with her during which I usually got various critical remarks off my chest.

My mother—she did not wish to be addressed as "Mama," but only as "Mutter"—had a very slender figure all her life and a certain elegance of manner. She was a born journalist who expressed herself very quickly and aptly. At a time when women were not yet admitted to such professions she undoubtedly missed her vocation, for she would have been perfectly suited to a publishing career. She wrote magnificent letters, often lengthy feuilletons, and with a girl's fancy penmanship; I have preserved several bundles of her later letters to Jerusalem. In addition, she was the indispensable family poet, producing with the greatest ease poems and family plays which her four sons performed at various weddings and other functions between 1903 and 1908. On such occasions I was particularly annoyed that I, as the youngest, usually had to appear as a girl and wear the finery of my cousin Margot, who was about my age. My mother read quite a bit, too, especially novels and poems, with her repertory extending from Schiller to Richard Dehmel and Emile Verhaeren, the Flemish poet who had been translated into German by Stefan Zweig (sometimes quite well) and who was widely read at the time. She claimed that George and Rilke were beyond her.

Sometimes I also derived great benefit from her literary talent. When I was in the upper grades, she took an interest in the subjects of my essays, and whenever she found one to her liking, she would say: "I'll do that one." And she really did an excellent job. In the spring of 1914, when I was already an ardent student of Judaica and spent my free time studying Hebrew, the students in the penultimate year of the Gymnasium were given the theme for a major essay, which we were supposed to write at home over the next three or four weeks: "The Rhine as a Witness of German Life." The topic was not to my taste at all, but my mother was delighted. "Leave that to me," she said. "But you have to mention the persecution of the Jews in the First Crusade, when the communities in Mainz, Worms, and Speyer were slaughtered!" To that she had no objection, and so she wrote for me an enormously lyrical monologue of "Father Rhine" which described everything that had happened by the river's banks and ended with a pathos-filled hymn to labor by Verhaeren: *"Arbeit ist Stimme tiefsten Gebets | Er, der alles versteht, er versteht's | Sucht ihn im Schaffen."* [Labor is the voice of profound prayer. He, who understands everything, understands this. Seek him in labor]. I received an A "for the often poetic form" and kept the notebook as a souvenir. "Where did you find these beautiful verses?" asked my German teacher.

Mother had a very happy disposition as well as a flexibility that permitted her to adapt herself to any company or environment without great inhibitions or difficulties. At first this produced conflicts between us, for I frequently accompanied her on social calls and had to notice that at different places she unblushingly expressed opinions that were contradictory but pleased her hosts. My character was in the formative stage, so there was no dearth of objections on my part, and to these she replied with a sentence that still rings in my ears: *"Mein Sohn, moniere mich nicht."* [My son, don't you admonish me]. Only much later, when there were serious conflicts concerning my brother Werner and me and she had to bear the brunt of these, did I understand her desire to be enveloped in peace and quiet. For this she made many sacrifices. I have already said that she had a happy disposition, but I was never really able to find out whether she was happy. She had a pronounced taste for travel, and as the family's prosperity grew, she could often afford to take trips two or three times a year. But she almost always traveled alone or with a lady friend; during summer vacations she would travel with us children, and later, after 1904, she traveled mostly with me and my brother Werner. Thus I went to Switzerland with her four times between 1909 and 1914, traveling to Lugano and Lake Brienz; the outbreak of World War I surprised us high up in the Maderaner Valley. My father would join us only for an occasional weekend, provided we were not too far from Berlin, or for the last week of the summer vacation.

My mother was understandably very popular in the wider family circle. This was due not only to her sunny disposition and her polished and witty manner of expression, but also to the fact that she was considerably older than the other uncles and aunts and yet never attached any importance to that fact, which meant that respect for an older person could easily turn into a relationship of trust. The conflicts concerning socialism, Zionism, and attitudes toward the First World War, which soon loomed so large in our lives, never caused her to take an impassioned or even definite stand on these matters. She had sympathy for every point of view and did not wish to tie herself down, or to be tied down, to any of them. I was far too passionate not to take offense at this attitude on numerous occasions, but it is a fact that my mother did a great deal for me, even under very difficult circumstances and at the risk of bitter marital disputes.

II

Jewish Milieu

THE MOST COLORFUL figure in my family circle was undoubtedly Uncle Theobald, a brother of my father and ten years his junior. As I have already mentioned, he was, prior to his marriage, the only Zionist in the family. In this generally very anti-Zionist circle he constituted the opposition, and long before I was old enough to think for myself he was the center of vehement arguments. Now and then my father's firm printed Jewish books as well, particularly fiction (notably for the S. Cronbach publishing house). For a number of years the printshop also did a Jewish weekly edited by a man with a strange dual profession. Max Albert Klausner was a man of considerable Hebrew and general Jewish learning who had come to Germany from Poland as a very young man and was quite well known as a Jewish writer and journalist. But in addition to this activity he worked for some years for the Foreign Office in confidential matters—whether on a full-time or part-time basis, I don't know. My mother later told me this in confidence. The *Israelitische*

Wochenschrift [Israelite Weekly] appeared until before the outbreak of the war. One good thing about this journal was that some of the regularly running advertisements were paid for not in cash, but in kind. Not only did the big encyclopedia *Meyers Konversationslexikon* arrive volume by volume, free of charge, but not infrequently we had such treats as "advertising sausage," as my mother called it. My mother's sister was a close friend of Klausner's daughters, and so these and many related publications of their father came into our house. The *Israelitische Wochenschrift* was, of course, strictly anti-Zionist.

Things were quite different with my uncle, who together with another brother had taken over Grandfather's firm. From 1905 on the Zionist organization was his biggest customer. Thus he printed the two official German-language journals of the movement, the *Jüdische Rundschau* [Jewish Review], the organ of the Zionist Association for Germany, which later played an important role in the history of German Jewry under the editorship of Robert Weltsch, one of the outstanding journalists of the age, and later, for a few years until the outbreak of the world war, *Die Welt* [The World], the central organ of the Zionist Organization, founded by Theodor Herzl. When I began to get interested in these things, I went to the Hauptstrasse in Schöneberg every few weeks in order to pick up the issues accumulated there.

My uncle was a scholar manqué. His great love was the study of history and ethnology, and in his apartment in Friedenau an oak bookcase was filled with books about the Far East, Japan, China, Tibet, and India, as well as Buddhism and Islam. It was he who gave me the *Buddhistischer Katechismus* by Subhadra Bhikschu (actually a solid citizen named Zimmermann), the first book that I read about a Far Eastern religion. Financial difficulties forced him to leave school at an early age and enter a business apprenticeship, something to which he gradually accommodated himself. For years all the Scholem brothers had attended the religious school of a small synagogue on Prinzenstrasse, but my uncle was the only one who did so with great pleasure and a certain amount of success. At least he acquired the ability to read Hebrew almost fluently if it was printed with vowel marks, though he probably did not understand a great deal of what he read aloud—for example, what he chanted in the traditional singsong at the Seder. He looked very much like his father, but he had inherited his mother's energy, intelligence, and thrift. Although he expressed his views with resoluteness, he was always concerned about the preservation of family harmony—something that was certainly not easy in our case, especially given the great difference in age between him and my father. To him Zionism was a kind of spiritual liberation that manifested itself in a somewhat paradoxical way. He was one of the founders of the Jewish gymnastics association Bar Kochba and performed for Theodor Herzl at the Basel Zionist Congress of 1903. A photo of the squad of gymnasts with Herzl in the middle hung in the parlor of his home.

My uncle was quite a character. To my ears his opposition to his brothers manifested itself not so much in ideological disputes, which evidently had taken place long before I grew up, but in the Jewish expressions and solecisms in which he used to indulge on Friday evenings. Their mixed reception on the part of some of the congregants only seemed to inspire him to further productions of linguistic Jewishness. In my parents' generation, the Jewish petite bourgeoisie still frequently used such expressions in private conversation as a matter of course, though they were hardly ever used in public. At our Friday evening gatherings my uncle bandied them about like watchwords, as it were. In his home the collection box of the Jewish National Fund for the acquisition of land in Palestine hung in a prominent place. When he won a bet he had made with his brothers, it usually was paid by throwing a one-mark piece into this box.

In the gymnastics association, which was supposed to give concrete expression to the "Judaism of muscles," Max Nordau's dreadful formula for the physical regeneration of the Jews, this man, who represented nothing of the sort, found a relaxation that was rather incomprehensible to me. The formula bothered me from the beginning, and although my uncle kept inviting me to join once I had shown an interest in Zionism, I could never bring myself to satisfy my Jewish enthusiasm, which thirsted for knowledge and insight, with gymnastics. That is why my uncle seemed to become more problematical to me as I grew up. I felt much human sympathy for his contradictory nature, but my annoyance at what seemed to me the unrealistic plane of his Zionism made me increasingly nervous. Yet I very much appreciated the fact that he took my side during the war, when my attitude brought me into grave conflict with my father. That sort of thing could not be taken for granted in those days. I felt really close to his wife, Aunt Hedwig, who was my main support in the family and who gladly stood behind my inclinations, which were still unclear but tended in the direction of spiritual Zionism. She was still in her twenties when I began to form these inclinations, and a genuine relationship of trust developed between us. During the war years and even later I often went out to Friedenau for the noonday meal, and when my uncle lay down for a nap I used to discuss with my aunt all my concerns in connection with my Jewish endeavors. Shortly after the war she took a young girl into her home to help her care for her two small children, my much younger cousins Eva and Dinah. Esther Dondikoff, who spoke Hebrew fluently, came from one

of the first Jewish villages in Eretz Yisrael and had come
to Berlin for training as a kindergarten teacher. She taught
my aunt Hebrew and sang to the little girls the Hebrew
songs then in vogue in her country. Later she became the
wife of Moshe Smilansky, one of the most respected men
of Jewish Palestine, who worked for Jewish-Arab understanding for many years and with great energy.

When I told my aunt that I had decided to go to Palestine, she was delighted and said she would like to go
herself. But that idea ran up against the calculations
of my uncle, a cautious businessman who did not think
that he could successfully transplant his rather large
print shop over there. Those were plans of the early
twenties which sometimes came under discussion before
my own emigration.

At this point I should like to say something about the
phenomenon of assimilation which loomed so large in the
life of German Jewry in my youth. A great variety of factors were involved there. At the beginning of this century
any young Jew who was not part of the strictly Orthodox
minority faced the progressive deterioration of his Jewish
identity. There was something in the atmosphere that
came from the environment, something conscious that
dialectically combined a desire for self-relinquishment
with a desire for human dignity and loyalty to one's own
self; there was a deliberate break with the Jewish tradition, of which the most varied and often peculiar frag-
ments were still present in atomized form; and there was
also a drifting (not always conscious) into a world which
was to replace that tradition. As for the kind of world
this would be, this was subject to the same totally different
views that prevailed in the non-Jewish environment. The
hope for social emancipation (which was supposed to fol-
low the political emancipation completed in 1867–70), in

part also the outright hope for full integration and absorption in the German people—a hope that was largely shared and encouraged by the non-Jewish champions of this emancipation—was in conflict with the general experience of rising anti-Semitism. Only wishful thinking could suppress that experience, although there were varying degrees of awareness of the conflict. We cannot disregard these factors today; they were understandable in the context of the times and had a significant effect. And yet there was an even crueler factor of which only those were aware (and there were quite a few of them) who achieved some detachment from this phenomenon, whether through trauma or through slow evolution. I am referring to self-deception, and its discovery was one of the most decisive experiences of my youth. Most Jews lacked discrimination in all matters affecting themselves, yet in all other matters they mustered that faculty for reasoning, criticism, and vision which others have justifiably admired or criticized in them. This capacity for self-deception is one of the most important and dismal aspects of the German-Jewish relationship. It is shocking to observe the foolhardy efforts being made today to play it down. Jewish humor, in fact, was capable of seeing through this self-deception, or perhaps the humor was the only thing that made it bearable in most people's consciousness. The number of Jewish jokes that belong in this category is legion. Today, to be sure, it is hard to read with equanimity the writers who expressed this kind of widespread self-deception, including such important figures as Hermann Cohen, Fritz Mauthner, and Constantin Brunner, the grandson of a chief rabbi of Hamburg. There is something unreal about this literature, and the sad thing is that this is not only apparent today, when everything is over and done with, but could have been perceived even then, when such writers were still being cheered. This kind of self-deception also acted as a form of censorship—though I cannot entirely say whether it was conscious or unconscious—of scholarly publications on the history of the Jews in Germany. I still remember the indignation with which I read many contributions to the *Zeitschrift für die Geschichte der Juden in Deutschland* [Journal for the History of the Jews of Germany], a periodical once edited by Ludwig Geiger, an associate professor of German literature at the University of Berlin and the son of Abraham Geiger, one of the three most important Jewish scholars in Germany in the nineteenth century. There self-censorship may actually be observed as a method. But one thing is clear: the large segments of German Jewry under discussion here, and their intellectual and political representatives, *wanted* to believe in assimilation with, and integration into, an environment that by and large viewed the Jews at best with indifference and at worst with malevolence. It is also true that to a certain degree (and this is something on which judgments today differ) the German environment encouraged and welcomed this process, while other strong elements in the population felt disturbed and disquieted by it. How far this went is shown by a very characteristic statement made by Werner Sombart, a very famous sociologist and economist of the time who was torn between liberal and antiliberal views. When this statement was published and widely quoted in 1912, it created a tremendous stir among the Jews. It said that while the legal equality and emancipation of the Jews should not be formally abrogated, Jews should voluntarily refrain from making use of these rights in public life. Coming before the First World War, this statement was a stronger storm signal than all the others coming from the ranks of the Pan-Germans and the outright anti-Semites.

In many ways the life-style of the assimilated Jews with whom I grew up was a confused jumble. For example, the picture of Theodor Herzl that hung in my room in Berlin and Munich for many years came into my possession in a strange way. Since the days of my grandparents, when this confusion had started, Christmas was celebrated in our family—with roast goose or hare, a decorated Christmas tree which my mother bought at the market by St. Peter's Church, and the big distribution of presents for servants, relatives, and friends. It was asserted that this was a German national festival, in the celebration of which we joined not as Jews but as Germans. An aunt who played the piano treated our cook and servant girl to "Silent Night, Holy Night." Naturally, as a child this made sense to me, and the last time I participated in it was in 1911, when I had just begun to study Hebrew. Under the Christmas tree there was the Herzl picture in a black frame, and my mother said: "We selected this picture for you because you are so interested in Zionism." From then on I left the house at Christmastime.

Christmas was not celebrated at my uncle's home, of course. Instead, he celebrated Chanukah, the Jewish feast of lights from which the Church derived Christmas. The festival owes its origin to the victory of the Maccabees in their uprising against the King of Assyria's attempts at Hellenization (thus against "assimilation"!) and to the cleansing of the temple in Jerusalem of Greek idols— and the Zionist movement really played up the occasion. On Christmas Eve, mostly for the benefit of the many unmarried young men and girls who did not wish to participate in their parents' Christmas celebrations, the so-called Maccabean Ball was held—a peculiar invention about which the Maccabees presumably would have had a thing or two to say (which is also true of some other things that were later perpetrated in their name). When I visited my uncle at Chanukah in one of the war years and asked his daughters who had given them all those beautiful presents, they replied, "Our good Father Chanukah brought them to us." Although no Chanukah candles were lit in our home and the very popular Hebrew song that goes with the ceremony was not sung, my uncle always called on us and, ironically enough, brought my parents and me a package of gingerbread each as well as a braided challah with poppy seeds on top in place of the popular Christmas stollen.

Baptism was no problem in these circles. In the history of the Scholem and Hirsch families there were only two baptisms between 1831 and 1933, the years for which documentation was available to me—both of girls between twenty and thirty who were named Therese Scholem. One of these, who survived World War II in Pasing (near Munich) as the wife of a Catholic soldier, returned to the Jewish fold as soon as there was a rabbi in Munich again. On the other hand, mixed marriages became a growing problem, particularly from about 1900 on. As early as the beginning of the 1890s one of my mother's cousins married a Gentile, though she remained Jewish herself. Her husband, to be sure, deserted her a few years later. As a consequence, their two daughters Irma and Lony (one of whom later became a good friend of mine), who presumably had been baptized at birth, grew up in a completely Jewish milieu and all their lives did not quite know where they really belonged.

Twenty years later there was another mixed marriage, and its history was memorable enough. In 1911 my mother's sister, whom I have already mentioned as one of the first female doctors admitted to practice in Berlin, at the age of thirty-eight married a colleague who was ten years her junior. Her parents were no longer alive at the time, and the man's parents were bitterly opposed to their son's marrying a Jewish woman. The man always remained a stranger to our family. Everybody was extremely polite and infinitely obliging toward one another, but there was no warmth, and husband and wife largely confined themselves to their own company. They lived in an ivory tower in Friedenau, practically around the corner from my Zionist uncle, and yet there never was any contact between them. The little house that they rented was full of Far Eastern art: Buddhas and Kwanyins were everywhere. Everything was culture, culture and more culture, and high-class journals, from the *Neue Rundschau* [New Review] to the *Sozialistische Monatshefte* [Socialist Monthly], seemed to be their daily fare. They associated with each other and a small circle of friends consisting entirely of Jews, but only those who tried to make little or no use of their Jewishness. My mother and her brother Hans Hirsch often went to see them, only rarely accompanied by one of us children; but when she came home she often heaved a sigh, without expanding further on the issue. The big test came in 1933. After a while my uncle discovered, following a marriage of more than twenty years, that he was an "Aryan" and asked my aunt Käthe to release him so he could marry a German. Thus my aunt was later taken to the ghetto of Theresienstadt, where she died.

The issue of mixed marriages in my family grew thornier when my brother Werner, who later became a Communist deputy in the Reichstag, married his girlfriend Emmy Wiechelt, a member of the Sozialistische Arbeiterjugend [Young Socialist Workers] in Hannover, toward the end of the first war. My mother did not mind this, and for as long as the new family lived in Berlin (in the back wing of a building in the largely Jewish Hansa district) she frequently visited them. My father, whose ideology ought to have made him welcome a mixed marriage, declined after a brief formal encounter to have any further contact with my brother and his daughter-in-law. I had quite a good relationship with my sister-in-law, who was also active as a Communist for a long time. But who could describe my astonishment when many years later, in the 1960s, she asked me: "Why didn't Werner bring me into the Jewish fold?" I replied: "But the two of you were Communists, and he left the Jewish fold just as you left the Church!" "No matter," she said with a naiveté that I never understood but that protected her all her life. "It would have been the right thing to do." One year before her death she converted to Judaism because she wanted at least to be buried among Jews.

When the phonograph became popular in Germany at the beginning of this century, my father tried to get orders to print labels for the records, and he was quite successful in his quest. He purchased several of the requisite stamping presses, and at home he often told us proudly that he was supplying about half the labels of all records manufactured in Germany. This idea contributed greatly to increasing our prosperity. In wartime, when the bureaucracy proliferated mightily, he had another very successful idea. He noticed the proliferation of printed forms, and he established a "forms division" of which he was the sole owner and which he kept busy printing the many forms that were needed, having obtained the texts and the orders from the proper authorities. As the war brought about the loss of many customers and orders, this initiative enabled him to get through the war years. He had hoped for help after 1914 from my two oldest brothers, Reinhold and Erich, whom he had for years diligently trained to succeed him in business, but they were drafted into the army and he had to bear the main

burden himself, which in view of his worsening arterio-
sclerosis meant a double strain. These two brothers had
been sent for further training to print shops in Paris
and London that were doing business with us, and so
I had little contact with them during the years of my
most decisive development, 1909 to 1920, and practically no contact with my oldest brother Reinhold. Thus
I established a closer relationship only with my brother
Werner, who was two years older than I and had a very
volatile disposition which brought him into opposition
to our parental home at an early age. This prompted my
parents around 1908 to send him for two or three years
to the Samson School at Wolfenbüttel, a Jewish boarding school associated with a Realschule that had been
founded a hundred years previously when Westphalia
was a kingdom. Many Jewish businessmen, cattle dealers,
and master butchers in Western Germany sent their children to that school. There my brother encountered a
considerable amount of religious hypocrisy and false
patriotism, which he found quite repulsive. The school
was run along strict German nationalistic lines, but some
major aspects of the Jewish ritual, daily prayer and a
kosher kitchen, were maintained. During school vacations I would be treated to cynical lectures and outpour-
ings on the subject of his school by my brother, who was
beginning to test his rhetorical skills on me even then.
He finally managed to be brought back home to Berlin,
but two years later another row erupted. While I shot
up to a considerable height, my brother remained rather
small, but at an early date he developed sharp intellectual facial features which clearly reflected his nature.
During our adolescent years we were to be faced with
various shocks and conflicts. They pointed us in entirely
different directions, yet again and again they brought us
closer to each other.

In those prewar years Berlin was still basically a very quiet city. In my early school years we would leave from the Kupfergraben on the horse-drawn streetcar to visit my mother's parents and reach Charlottenburg via the Tiergarten, which was still a real, large park. Only half the city was paved with asphalt, and in many parts of it, expecially in the east and the north, horsecars still rattled over cobblestones. The first autobuses were a great sensation, and to climb on the upper deck was a coveted pleasure. This all became apparent to me at the time when rollerskates came into fashion (around 1909) and I began to explore Berlin on them during the summer months. No policeman stopped a boy of twelve or thirteen from threading his way through the tangle of carriages, automobiles, and electric streetcars on the busiest streets, of which there were not that many. Only at a small number of especially difficult intersections, such as Friedrichstrasse, Leipziger Strasse, and Unter den Linden, were the feeble beginnings of traffic control in evidence. Thus I rollerskated my way through the asphalted parts of Berlin, the length and the breadth of it, usually in the late afternoon.

Around that time, in September of 1910, I sold all my children's books to a secondhand book dealer on Wallstrasse in a fit of defiance which I greatly regretted later, because I had decided to set up a "real" library. I was greatly interested in history, even before my mathematical inclinations also asserted themselves. The awakening of the latter was due to the influence of my marvelous longtime mathematics teacher, Franz Goldscheider, whose brother was a famous physician. He was the only teacher in my school who meant anything to me. (To him I owe my early acquaintance with Laurence Sterne's *Tristram Shandy*.)

In our bookcase there were the nineteen volumes of Friedrich Christoph Schlosser's *Weltgeschichte* [World

History], one of the main works of liberal and reasonably popular historiography in German. I devoured this work in its entirety, which is more than I can say of the two rows of classics (published by Meyers Bibliographisches Institut) on the shelves above the Schlosser. These contained too many things that could not attract a growing boy. However, I began to buy volumes of the Reclam-Bibliothek series, each of which cost twenty pfennigs, and the Sammlung Göschen, of which a clothbound volume—they were on every possible subject—cost eighty pfennigs. Of these series I bought primarily works on history as well as translations of the classical historians, later also treatments of special mathematical fields with which I had become aquainted at school. I read a great many historical works before I picked up my first novel.

My parents were busy at the printshop, where my mother did the bookkeeping, so that we children—and particularly I, as the youngest—were on our own. My freedom was curtailed in 1910 for about a year only by the semiweekly visits of Mademoiselle Girardot, a spinster from Geneva who was supposed to teach me piano and conversational French, since my mother did not deem the French instruction just starting then at school to be sufficient. The piano lessons were a total fiasco, and at school I was excused from music instruction as a so-called *"Brummer"* [tin ear], for my voice was unpleasantly conspicuous when we sang those beautiful Protestant chorales. On the other hand, the walks (this time really on foot) along the Spree to the Museumsinsel [Museum Island] or to the Tiergarten did leave some traces of French conversation. After about a year I managed to scare my teacher away, whereupon she left me as a souvenir her scarecrow photo with this inscription: *"Vous m'aimerez quand je n'y serai plus et vous m'écrirez cela"* [You will love me when I am no longer here and will write to tell me so]. But it never came to pass. She was the only "governess" I ever had. Since school was child's play for me, I had a lot of free time. I cannot remember any attempts of my father or my mother to steer me in any definite direction in those years. Since I brought home such good report cards, I seemed to be no problem and could be left to my own devices. Of course, I frequently had to accompany my mother when she went shopping, particularly in the stores on Leipziger Strasse, or visiting. I can still picture her wearing a big plumed hat and a boa.

III

Jewish
Awakening (1911–1914)

THE FIRST IMPETUS for my Jewish consciousness was provided by my interest in history. Our school's instruction in Jewish religion, which did not even enable pupils to read Hebrew and was in any case not required after age fourteen, offered me hardly any stimulation, and my parents had sent none of us four to the optional religious school maintained by the Jewish Community Council, where I would probably have learned a bit more. The selections from Auerbach's *Israelitische Hausbibel* that we read in religion class, and the teacher's very cursory explanations of the Jewish holidays (of which, as I have already said, I experienced very little at home), did not make much of an impression on me. It later turned out that this boring Dr. Moses Barol was really a very learned man from Odessa who was employed as a librarian at the Lehranstalt für die Wissenschaft des Judentums [Teaching Institution for the Science of Judaism], the Reform rabbinical seminary. But he lacked pedagogical passion. One day in summer 1911 he showed us the three fat volumes that constituted the popular edition of Heinrich Graetz's eleven-volume *Geschichte der Juden* [History of the Jews], indisputably one of the most important works of Jewish historiography. When I asked Dr. Barol where I could read this work, he referred me to the very important library of the Jewish Community Council on Oranienburger Strasse, where adolescents like myself could get a card if they brought a note from their father or mother (my mother readily gave me one) vouching for their offspring. For years I was among the most zealous users of this library, which was later destroyed by the Nazis.

It is thus that I came to read this voluminous work, which was not only exceedingly rich in often dramatic information, but also was written in an impressive, vivid, and readable style. I devoured those volumes with great interest, and then requested them as a bar mitzvah present from my parents and my uncle along with Theodor Mommsen's four-volume *Römische Geschichte* [History of Rome]. The religious coming of age, which according to Jewish precepts begins at age thirteen, had in the nineteenth century degenerated among nonobservant Jews into an imitation of the Protestant confirmation, provided that the ceremony was observed at all (and it was still widely observed). A popular Jewish proverb has it that every Jew has his own *Shulhan Arukh*—the codification of the Jewish religious law from the sixteenth century which governs religious practices. My father, who was otherwise not observant at all, had decided that we were still too immature at age thirteen and thus postponed the celebration until the Sabbath before our fourteenth birthday—a strange bit of private theology. Following the general custom of the time, Father went to the synagogue wearing a top hat. The bar mitzvah boy was called to the Torah for the first (and in many cases the last) time and had to say two brief Hebrew benedictions before and after, whereupon the rabbi admonished him before the congregation to be loyal to Judaism and its ideals. At home the boy in most cases received from his relatives the foundation of a future library, chiefly in the form of editions of the classics (which, to be sure, were often sold quickly enough). Usually a rabbinical student was hired to prepare a boy for the bar mitzvah, as was done in the case of my brothers, and this tutor was supposed to teach the boy a few Jewish precepts and rituals in addition to drumming the Hebrew text of the benedictions into him. My brothers, who could not read Hebrew, wrote down the text in transliteration.

In my case, however, a shift had occurred. The profound impression which Graetz's work had made upon me instilled in me the desire to learn Hebrew. Thus I went to see our religion teacher after the summer vacation together with my classmate Edgar Blum, who was a close friend of mine (he fell in World War I, on his twentieth birthday), and asked him whether he was prepared to help us acquire a reading knowledge of Hebrew as well as the fundamentals of the language itself. Dr. Barol was very pleased and gave us an additional hour of instruction twice a week after school. Since we really wanted to learn, we progressed very quickly, and I informed my parents that I did not need a tutor for my bar mitzvah because I had decided to learn Hebrew. My father received this disclosure about the same way as he would have if I had told him that I wanted to take Greek lessons at home, and complimentary ones at that. But it was not long before he realized that he had gotten more than he had bargained for.

After a few months our private lessons with Dr. Barol were discontinued, and since I did not know anyone I could turn to, I tried to go on by myself. My friend Edgar Blum, whose mother had sent him to a religious school, told me that one did not learn nearly enough there and could spend one's time quite differently in intensive study. Thus I bought myself Hebrew grammars and books of exercises and taught myself for about fifteen months. My father only shook his head.

At that time I began to attend the Berlin synagogues regularly, particularly for the Friday evening services which were still held almost entirely in Hebrew even in the so-called Reform synagogues, where there was organ accompaniment. The difference between the Reform and the Conservative rites was, in addition to unimportant cuts and the organ music, the elimination of all references to the return of the people of Israel to the Holy Land and the replacement of these references by "universally human" asseverations. Since I quickly learned to understand the texts of the prayers and rather liked the organ accompaniment of the liturgy, I found attendance at the synagogue impressive and pleasurable. It gave me a chance to check on the progress of my Hebrew studies, for I had begun to study by myself not only portions of the Hebrew Bible but the texts of the old prayer book as well. The strictly Orthodox services at the Alte Synagoge attracted me even more than the organ synagogue on Lindenstrasse, which was not far from our home. The Alte Synagoge was located on Heidereuthergasse, a small street next to the Neuer Markt where most of the Jews had settled after their readmission to Berlin in 1671 and where a great many Jews still were living. Here there was neither an organ nor a women's choir, and the old ritual impressed me greatly. A major contributory factor was the wonderful Hebrew chanting of the chief cantor, the "royal music director" Aron Friedmann, whose singing went straight to the heart. Since most of those attending this synagogue understood the text of the prayers and took an active part in the service, there was a rapport between the cantor and the worshippers that was not easily found elsewhere. Some other synagogues also had cantors with fantastic vocal gifts—a number of great opera and concert singers, such as Hermann Jadlowker and Joseph Schmidt in my time, came from their ranks—but their presentation suggested the atmosphere of an operatic production more than that of a religious rite.

Not far from that synagogue, on Neue Friedrichstrasse, were the two most important dealers in secondhand Judaica where I gained my first experience with Jewish books and began to buy, as far as my wallet permitted, books and pamphlets about Judaism and its history, and later Hebrew texts as well. Thus my passion for things Jewish, past and present, was born. It was no miracle that now, starting in 1911, I began to read Zionist literature, the writings of Moses Hess, Leon Pinsker, Theodor Herzl, Max Nordau, and Nathan Birnbaum (who originated the word *Zionism*), and confronted my parents with this interest.

This aroused the vehement opposition of my father, who belonged to the strictly anti-Zionist Centralverein deutscher Staatsbürger jüdischen Glaubens [Central Association of German Citizens of the Jewish Faith], and the discussions at our family table became heated.

In my parents' bookcase there were some Hebrew books somewhere on the back shelves as well as other Hebrew books from the estate of my great-grandparents, particularly of David Schlesinger, a very pious man who had received a thorough Hebrew education. Otherwise I remember only two Jewish works of fiction that were very popular at the time, Israel Zangwill's *The King of Schnorrers* and the collection *Jüdische Witze* [Jewish Jokes] by Herrmann Noël. I thought the latter book was magnificent, and to this day I feel that it is noteworthy as

one of the best-formulated collections in the German
language, vastly superior to certain horrible products of
that type that are available today and that can only cause a
reader familiar with things Jewish no end of astonishment
and annoyance.

In 1912 there was a brief period in the life of my
brother Werner (who had returned to Berlin) when he
was attracted to the political aspect of Zionism, though
he did not really make a commitment to it. Even though he
joined the Sozialdemokratische Arbeiterjugend [Young
Social Democratic Workers] toward the end of that year,
it was through him that I became acquainted with a group
of like-minded young people who had also joined the
Zionist movement during their last years in school. It was
called "Jung Juda" [Young Judea]. My brother wrote
them a letter saying that he had found a broader, more
comprehensive sphere of activity and could no longer be
active in their midst. He and I came to blows because he
tried to force me to listen to socialist speeches of his own
devising, which he delivered to an imaginary audience
while standing on a chair—an enterprise that I resolutely
opposed. He recommended to me the writings of Bebel
and Kautsky, *Die Lessinglegende* by Franz Mehring, as well
as various pamphlets. I kept Konrad Haenisch's anthology
of proletarian poetry and Adolf Hoffmann's *Die Zehn
Gebote und die besitzenden Klassen* [The Ten Commandments and the Propertied Classes], a pamphlet immensely
popular at the time, for more than thirty years, until I
decided I could live without them. Historical materialism,
the most massive forms of which made so much sense to
my brother that he would have loved to pound them into
me, was now very far removed from the historical and
philosophical interests and inclinations that shaped my
own development.

My brother's Berlin activities came to an end when he was going on eighteen. One day in 1913 my father came into his office and found that one of the typesetters had placed on his desk a clipping of an item from the socialist daily *Vorwärts* about my brother's activity in the Arbeiterjugend. Coming from his own firm, this act, which was evidently intended as an ironic comment on the "capitalist employer," made my father very angry. After a great deal of trouble it was agreed that my brother, who was then in his final year of secondary school, would leave Berlin and attend Gildemeister's Institute in Hannover (a cram school to prepare for the final examination as an "extern," or a *"Presse,"* as such a school was then called). Ernst Jünger, the novelist, was his fellow pupil there for a year. Many years later Jünger told me that after sixty years he still vividly remembered my brother, with whom he had often conversed.

Perhaps one can say that the very different directions in which we four brothers developed in the ensuing years were typical of the world of the Jewish bourgeoisie and demonstrated what little influence a seemingly common environment has on the path taken by an individual young person. My oldest brother Reinhold, who at the time of the abovementioned disputes was on a year's military duty with a signal battalion, became a rightist, if anything, and displayed even stronger assimilationist tendencies than my father. Later he became a member of the *Deutsche Volkspartei* [German People's Party], and if the *Deutschnationale* [German nationalists] had welcomed Jews as members, he probably would have joined them. In 1938 he emigrated to Australia, and when we had a reunion with him in Zurich shortly after his eightieth birthday, my wife, who was not well versed in these German matters, asked him what he really was. He answered, perhaps overdoing it a bit: "I am a *Deutschnationaler.*" "What?"

said my wife, "and you say that after Hitler?" "I'm not going to let Hitler dictate my views to me!" he replied. That left her speechless. And yet I had implored her beforehand never to start a political discussion with him, as it would lead nowhere; each person had to respect the boundaries of the other. My second brother completed the picture. For a time he was a member of the "Democratic Club" and walked in the footsteps of my parents, particularly my mother—which is to say that he desired his peace more than anything and tried to commit himself as little as possible. Yet there was an age span of only six years between the four of us.

Between 1912 and 1917, and even later when I was in Berlin, I was very active in the Jung Juda association. Most of us went to Palestine at the beginning of the twenties after attending agricultural training schools, particularly the one at the Markenhof near Freiburg im Breisgau, an estate whose Jewish proprietor supported the vocational retraining championed by the Zionists. Later these emigrant pioneers were the founding members of Bet Zera in the Jordan valley, a kibbutz which flourished after some difficult years. I was in close touch with these members for years, and still am in touch with some of them today.

The members of Jung Juda consisted in part of children from the same assimilated group that I came from, but there were also sons of families that were still fully or partly observant, as well as a number of sons of Eastern European parentage who had grown up in Germany. The largest representation was made up of boys from the upper classes of the Sophiengymnasium, which had an especially high percentage of Jewish pupils. I was particularly interested in the members from Eastern Europe, and this interest was shared by others. The more we

encountered the not at all infrequent rejection of Eastern
European Jewry in our own families, a rejection that
sometimes assumed flagrant forms, the more strongly we
were attracted to this very kind of Jewishness. I am not
exaggerating when I say that in those years, particularly
during the war and shortly thereafter, there was something like a cult of Eastern Jews among the Zionists. All
of us had read Martin Buber's first two volumes about
Hasidism, *The Tales of Rabbi Nachman* and *The Legend of
the Baal Shem*, which had appeared a few years earlier and
had made Buber very famous. In every Jew we encountered from Russia, Poland, or Galicia we saw something
like a reincarnation of the Baal Shem Tov or at any rate
of an undisguised Jewishness that fascinated us. These
contacts and friendships with Eastern European Jews
have played a great role in my life.

One branch of Jung Juda met in a café at the Tiergarten
railway station. There the pupils of West Berlin secondary
schools held their discussions and scheduled lectures,
including a discussion with the circle around Gustav
Wyneken's periodical *Der Anfang* [The Beginning] in the
late fall of 1913. There I first saw and heard Walter
Benjamin as the main speaker. Around 1912 a further
branch covering the center and the east of Berlin had
been established, and it sponsored lectures every other
week in the large back room of the hotel Zur Goldenen
Gans [At the Sign of the Golden Goose]. Out of con-
sideration for the children of more traditional-minded
families, of whom there were even more in this section
than in the west, one of the two strictly kosher hotels in
the center of Berlin, located only a few minutes from the
Alte Synagoge, had been selected. The speakers were
predominantly students who viewed us as likely new
members of their wholly or partially Zionist-oriented
associations. There were discussions of books of Jewish

interest that had attracted general attention, such as
Arthur Schnitzler's *Der Weg ins Freie* [The Road to the
Open], probably the first novel by an important prose
writer in which the crisis of German-speaking Jewry in its
Viennese manifestation was described and presented for
general discussion with astonishing objectivity and inci-
siveness. There were recitations as well, for example
from the poetry of Else Lasker-Schüler, especially the
Hebräische Balladen which had just been published (in
1913). Some of these are among her most beautiful
and most unforgettable creations. (There is a wonderful
Hebrew translation of the brief, melancholy, and proud
poem "Mein Volk" [My People].) On other occasions,
stories by the great Jewish storytellers of Eastern Europe
were read in the Yiddish original or in German translation;
the Yiddish presentations, some of them magnificent,
by students from Lithuania or Byelorussia, made a profound impression. Events in Jewish life, such as the ritual-
murder trial of Mendel Beilis, a lowly brickyard employee,
which took place in Kiev on orders from the Czar and
created an enormous stir, gave rise to discussions and
analyses of their implications. In those years I also participated—probably the only time I did so in Germany—
in a huge public meeting at which some of the greatest
popular orators of the time, non-Jews as well as Jews,
protested against that shameful trial. This inspired me to
make a decision that practically none of my associates,
then or later, shared: I began to read old and new anti-
Semitic literature—first in connection with that trial and
then anti-Jewish writings generally. Among these were
periodicals like Theodor Fritzsch's *Der Hammer,* which
twenty years before Hitler's accession to power clearly
and unmistakably propagated everything that the Nazis
later translated into action. After I had delved into writings
of this kind, I realized early on that it was pointless to have

discussions of an apologetic nature unless these related to such clearly delineated phenomena as the accusation of ritual murder. At an early stage I developed an aversion to apologetic activities on the part of Jews. The Zionists' attitude in this regard made sense to me, and I am sure it indirectly influenced my later work, which was devoted to the objective investigation and analysis of phenomena which were unaccounted for and conflicted with the apologetic Jewish historiography of the day. At that time, to be sure, I had no way of knowing this.

However, my study of Hebrew and the Biblical and post-Biblical sources claimed far more of my free time than the above pursuits. These studies extended in particular from 1915 to my emigration. I was fortunate in that three or four of us from the Jung Juda group found a teacher who was nothing short of ideal in the rabbi of a small Orthodox private synagogue on Dresdenerstrasse to which the father of one of our group belonged. This teacher, to whom I for one owe infinitely much, was Dr. Isaak Bleichrode (1867–1954), a great-grandson of Rabbi Akiba Eger, who was probably the greatest Talmudic scholar in Germany at the beginning of the nineteenth century. Bleichrode, whose father was the author of a Hebrew-language biography of Akiba Eger, was a quiet and very pious man with an uncommonly relaxed and friendly manner. The only strange thing about him was that he never married, something that one does not usually like to see in the case of a rabbi. He was once very much in love in his youth, and when he could not get the girl, who was from a wealthy family, he decided to remain single. He was hardly what one would call a great scholar, but even within his limitations he was the first true personification of a *"Schriftgelehrter"* [Biblical scholar] that I encountered, and if I may say so, he was my living model for what that really is. He was a wonderful teacher, one who was able to elucidate a page of the Talmud. Some of us came from quite irreligious homes, and yet he welcomed us with all his heart and without any reservations. Nor did he ever make any attempt to influence our outlook on life; instead, he relied on the "light of the Torah" which he kindled for us. We were his best pupils, and perhaps his pedagogical genius caught fire precisely from us who were alienated from Judaism. He died at a ripe old age in Jerusalem, and I spoke at his grave.

It sounds incredible when I say that before World War I the large and prosperous Jewish community of Berlin flatly refused to permit the establishment of a class in which Talmud and cognate studies would be taught, not even in one of the religious schools it maintained. When a proposal of this kind had been rejected yet again, a small number of teachers with a traditional orientation decided to start such a class without any remuneration at the religious school on Annenstrasse, less than ten minutes from our home. If I ask myself whether I ever had what one might call an *Erlebnis* [a living experience] in my relationship to things Jewish, I can give only one answer: it was the thrill I experienced on a Sunday in April 1913 when Bleichrode taught me to read the first page of the Talmud in the original, and later that same day the exegesis by Rashi, the greatest of all Jewish commentators, of the first verses of Genesis. It was my first traditional and direct encounter, not with the Bible, but with Jewish substance in tradition. In any case, this encounter shaped my admiration and affection for Judaica more than any other subsequent experience in this field. In those years we studied five or six hours every Sunday morning, and soon Bleichrode invited me to participate in a *shiur* [lesson] which he held in his home for two hours on two evenings a week for a few members of his congregation and where we "learned" an entire tractate of the Talmud. (One did not study the Talmud, one "learned" it.) Thus I "learned" with Bleichrode for four years, and I soon had other opportunities to participate in such courses, where a certain section of the Talmud was read with Rashi's commentary and sometimes also with the relevant further discussions of French rabbis of the twelfth and thirteenth centuries.

In those years there was a period during which I studied Hebrew for fifteen hours a week in addition to my school work. I can no longer say whether it was my enthusiasm that made this heavy work load easy for me or whether it was the contents of those unforgettable hours that inspired my enthusiasm. I need not dwell on the fact that I never paid as much as a penny for this instruction either then or later. None of my pious teachers would have accepted any payment for teaching a young person to "learn."

It is safe to say that the encounter with Judaism which I had in the years of my youth kindled my intellect and my imagination equally. But this encounter was far removed from the vision that crystallized after an occupation of fifty or sixty years with so many aspects of this phenomenon. What fascinated me in those days, the power of a tradition thousands of years old, was strong enough to shape my life and to cause me to progress from the absorption of a learner to that of a researcher and thinker. In the process, however, my vision of that tradition was changed decisively. Yet the change took place almost imperceptibly, so that I find it hard to reconstruct my original intuition of it. What I thought myself capable of grasping at the time—I filled many notebooks on the subject in my youth—became transformed as I grasped it, and the comprehension that I strove for turned into something that resisted conceptualization all the more emphatically the older I became; for it revealed a secret life, one which I had to acknowledge as being impossible to conceptualize, and which seemed portrayable only through symbols. But this later aspect of my efforts, which is, after all, the proper subject of my writings, cannot be discussed here.

Returning to my occupation with the Talmud and related literature, there were three things that particularly impressed me. One was the honesty with which traditions are preserved there that later editors might have censored, an honesty that occasionally staggers the reader. The utter naturalness with which all aspects of life were dealt with fascinated me. Then there was the laconism which I had been taught to admire in Latin class and which I encountered in much more pronounced form in these Hebrew and Aramaic texts of the Mishna, the Babylonian Talmud, and the Midrashim. The laconic brevity of those rabbis, their absolute precision of expression, attracted me even more than the same quality in the Latin writers. Added to this was the dialogue of the generations, uninterrupted for so many centuries, whose protocol is the Talmud. Here truly prevailed that "dialogic" life which the later Buber so emphatically placed at the center of his philosophy, although, paradoxically enough, he remained incomprehensibly blind to this, the most genuine evidence that Jewish tradition offered to him. The continuum of the Torah onto which all remarks of the "sages" and their disciples were projected was, in the final analysis, not a truly historical medium—the religious and metaphysical assumptions on which it was based, and with which I was later to concern myself extensively, were too evident for that—but it did have a dignity and, as I was soon to find out, problems of its own. My notes from that period of youthful reception indicate that I was of course not able

to state this so incisively at that time, but these were the
elements that caused me to read the classical documents
of rabbinic Judaism with reverence.

In those years, then, my extensive readings in German
literature—Jean Paul, Georg Christoph Lichtenberg, Paul
Scheerbart, Eduard Mörike, and Stefan George particularly attracted me—were increasingly supplemented with
the Bible, the Talmud, and the Midrash, texts whose
normative aspects appealed to me no less than their
imaginative ones. The many hours in which I became
acquainted with the discussions of the Halakhists and the
apothegms of the Aggadists profoundly influenced me.
However, after I had become thoroughly familiar with
the Orthodox way of life, I vacillated for years and finally
could not decide to embrace it. At any rate, the word
"Schriftgelehrter," which has a slightly derisive flavor in
non-Jewish literature, took on a very positive denotation
for me in my most impressionable years. During my
search for the tradition that had been lost to my circle, a
tradition that had a great magical attraction for me, the
writings of the ancient Jews seemed infinitely rich and
alive and in my consciousness bore comparison with the
very dissimilar world of the abovementioned German
authors, though on very different planes.

I have already mentioned the secondhand dealers in
Judaica whose shops I frequented, but not much less often
I rummaged among the treasures of a small bookshop on
Prinzenstrasse, two minutes from Dr. Bleichrode's apart-
ment. There, for a song, I bought the writings of Jean
Paul, Theodor Gottlieb von Hippel, Lichtenberg, and
Johann Georg Hamann. Other hunting grounds of my
virtually insatiable mania for learning, reading, and col-
lecting were the book carts next to the university where it
was possible, up to the early postwar years, to buy for next

to nothing the most abstruse and curious pamphlets and tomes. Thus I purchased for all of fifty pfennigs Lichtenberg's pseudonymously published satire from 1773 on Johann Caspar Lavater's attempt to convert Moses Mendelssohn, *Timorus, Vertheidigung zweyer Israeliten, die durch die Kräftigkeit der Lavaterischen Beweisgründe und der Göttingischen Mettwürste bewogen, den wahren Glauben angenommen haben* [Timorus, Defence of Two Israelites Who, Induced by the Power of Lavater's Arguments and Göttingen's Sausages, Have Accepted the True Faith]. This booklet is still on my shelves, and to my considerable satisfaction a copy was offered last year for fifteen hundred marks.

I was delighted to read the following sentence in an early edition of Lichtenberg: "Of all translations of my works that might be undertaken, I specifically request that they be translated into Hebrew!" And it was like a slap in the face when years later I read in Leitzmann's critical edition of Lichtenberg's *Sudelhefte* [Wastebooks] that my delight was based on a misprint and that the correct version reads not *"erbitte ich mir ausdrücklich"* [I specifically request] but *"verbitte ich mir ausdrücklich"* [I specifically prohibit]. And yet the incorrect version suited the tenor of Lichtenberg's writings as I perceived it then so much better. I did not become aware of the discordant notes of his late, rather anti-Jewish remarks until later. After re-examining the original manuscript, however, I would say that the correct meaning is still open to interpretation.

On a historical plane, the First World War was naturally the most important event of my youth. Today it is hard to imagine how profoundly everyone was affected by it, even one who had an entirely negative attitude toward its events. All around me the waves of enthusiasm for the war rose high. Only my brother Werner, with whom I exchanged many letters and who came back from Hannover toward the end of 1914 with a *Notabiturium* [secondary-school diploma issued under emergency conditions] in order to await his military orders in Berlin, shared my opposition to everything that was going on. From the outset he had belonged to that minority of the Social Democratic Party which later found its symbolic figures in Karl Liebknecht, Rosa Luxemburg, Georg Ledebur, and Hugo Haase. From my brother I learned that every two weeks there was an illegal meeting of this minority group in a restaurant in the Hasenheide in Neukölln at which one of its leaders would make a speech illuminating the events in the Socialist parties of the two war camps. I joined him in attending these meetings, where illegal pamphlets about war guilt and the like were distributed, and in April 1915 I took an active part in their dissemination. My last activity of this sort was the distribution of the Marxist journal *Die Internationale,* of which only one number appeared and which was immediately prohibited. Only when my brother was drafted into the army did I stop my visits to the Hasenheide.

To be sure, the Marxist doctrines that my brother now urged on me amicably rather than forcibly still impressed me far less than the writings of the anarchists, quite a few of which I read in the Berlin municipal library, prompted by the events of the day. There were, first of all, a remarkably calm and soberly written book by a Professor Paul Eltzbacher on the various trends of anarchism as well as the first brief biography of Bakunin by Nettlau. From there I went on to read Peter Kropotkin and Gustav Landauer, as well as Pierre Joseph Proudhon and Elisée Reclus. Their socialism was more meaningful to me than the supposedly scientific kind, which I never found convincing. Gustav Landauer's *Aufruf zum Sozialismus* [A

Call to Socialism] made a profound impression not only on me but on a considerable number of young Zionists as well. The same may be said of the personality of Landauer, who frequently lectured in those days before Zionist groups, and with whom I had several conversations toward the end of 1915 and in the following year. By that time I had already attempted to understand the three substantial volumes of Fritz Mauthner's *Beiträge zu einer Kritik der Sprache* [Toward a Critique of Language] to which an older student had directed my attention. Landauer, who was a great admirer and also a collaborator of Mauthner (though he made very negative remarks about the latter's attitude during the war), encouraged me to read his own observations and conclusions from Mauthner's theories which he had written down in his book *Skepsis und Mystik* [Skepticism and Mysticism]. Through Landauer I also established personal contact with the wholesale fur dealer Bernhard Mayer, whose offices were directly opposite our printshop on Beuthstrasse. Mayer, a very successful merchant who later lived in Switzerland for many years and played a major role as a patron of artists, writers, and persecuted politicians, had long been a confirmed anarchist and disciple of Kropotkin. He had left Brussels only because of the outbreak of the war, and spent only about two years in Berlin; during that time he handed me more anarchist literature. He and Landauer were very proud, conscious Jews who enjoyed discussions with Zionists, especially those who rejected the war and everything connected with it. In his later years Mayer became a virtual patron of Zionism, though he did not give up his convictions. Through influential groups from Russia the social and moral thought of anarchists like Tolstoi and Landauer has had an influence on the building of a new life in Eretz Yisrael that should not be underestimated. In the years under discussion here my own development moved markedly in this direction, though the chances of establishing an anarchistic society became ever more dubious to me. The optimistic assumptions about the nature of man on which all anarchist doctrines are based were subject to serious philosophical and historical doubts—unfortunately, I would say.

In this connection I should also say that the reason I embraced Zionism was not that the establishment of a Jewish state (which I defended in discussions) as the main goal of the movement seemed urgent and utterly convincing to me. For me as for many others, this aspect of the movement played only a secondary role, or none at all, until Hitler's destruction of the Jews. Those aspects of Zionism that dealt with politics and international law were not of prime importance to many of those who joined the movement. Of great influence, however, were tendencies that promoted the rediscovery by the Jews of their own selves and their history as well as a possible spiritual, cultural, and, above all, social rebirth. If there was any chance of a fundamental renewal whereby the Jews would fully realize their inherent potential, this—so we believed—could happen only over there, where a Jew would encounter himself, his people, and his roots. One's attitude toward religious tradition also played a part here, and had a clear dialectical function. For from the outset the struggle between a striving for continuation and revivification of the traditional form of Judaism and a conscious rebellion against this very tradition, though within the Jewish people and not through alienation from it and abandonment of it, created an ineluctable dialectics that was central to Zionism. Watchwords like "renewal of Judaism" or "revivification of the heart" only verbally masked this dialectics. It was bound to break through every attempt to endow it with substance in the concrete process of building a new Jewish community, and in large measure it shaped the inner history of the Zionist movement from my youth to the present.

In those years the most important spokesman of a Zionism determined culturally and socially and not by narrowly political considerations was the Hebrew essayist Asher Ginzberg in Russia, who became quite famous under the pseudonym Achad Ha'am ["one of the people"]. At that time his essays were being translated into German, and their very title, *Am Scheidewege* [At the Crossroads], alluded to the dialectics mentioned above. Continuity or a radical new start? Any attempt at mediating between these two positions was bound to remain questionable. Among the German-speaking Zionists, the most influential proponent of a radical new start undoubtedly was Martin Buber. In his *Reden über das Judentum* [Addresses on Judaism] he took Achad Ha'amism in a new, markedly religious-romantic direction, confronting a "religion" grown rigid in form with a "religiosity" that would be creative and truly central. Later Buber abandoned this antithesis, which was generally quite popular in Germany at that time, and struck out in different directions, but these would not contribute anything to an understanding of the powerful response evoked by his earlier speeches before Zionist youth groups. He found quite a few disciples who took up his catchword about *"Urjudentum,"* a primal Judaism that was to be retrieved from rigidified rabbinism. A number of publications in this vein, particularly the collection *Vom Judentum* [On Judaism], which was inspired by Buber and issued by Kurt Wolff in 1913, aroused violent controversies.

I was not mature enough to recognize clearly the fronts and the options that were concealed under so many formulas. It took me about two years to absorb all these impressions, and my mind was seething with a great

jumble of things. But I continued to be guided by a desire
to become familiar with the sources of the Jewish tradition. I was greatly impressed with Buber, but eventually I
defined myself as an adherent of Achad Ha'am, though I
remained indifferent to his agnostic philosophy, which he
had derived from Herbert Spencer. It was his great moral
seriousness that won me over.

In those years of vacillation, toward the end of 1913, I
joined a newly founded youth group of Agudat Yisrael
together with a few others from Jung Juda. I was even
made an officer, though I do not remember the maneuver
that got me elected. The Aguda was an Orthodox rival
organization of Zionism that had been founded in 1911
and at that time did not yet have its later ultra-clerical and
anti-Zionist orientation. Its programmatic statement—
"solution of all problems of contemporary Jewry in the
spirit of the Torah"—was an Orthodox imitation of the
Basel Program of Zionism, formulated in 1897, which
had defined as its goal the solution of the Jewish question
through "the establishment of a homeland in Palestine
secured under public law." I liked the new formulation of
the Aguda also, since I was certainly in sympathy with the
"spirit of the Torah." This formulation, however, was a
piece of Orthodox diplomacy, for what was meant was
not the "spirit of the Torah" but, much more precisely,
the letter of the *Shulhan Arukh,* the code of Jewish law.
In my case, that could not work out for long. To tell the
truth, the reason I joined this group was that it organized
an active program of intensive courses for the study of the
Hebrew sources. It was possible to participate in a whole
series of such courses at least five days a week from three
to nine. These courses were given by students and candidates for the rabbinate, some of them excellent. One of
them, a law student, even studied a brief Talmud tractate

with us, speaking to us in Hebrew. Although Zionism
was considered dangerous, it was tolerated. Our chairman, Leo Deutschländer, told me that Zionism was like
the ashes of the red heifer, which in accordance with
Num. 19:5 constituted an integral part of the ritual for
the cleansing of persons who had become unclean through
contact with human corpses. Like these ashes, Zionism
did manage to cleanse the unclean, but at the same time it
defiled the clean (namely those dealing with it). This
meant that it would point us "assimilationists" in the
direction of the Torah, but that the pious might run the
risk of being weaned away from the Torah by the modern
spirit prevailing in Zionism. As a matter of fact, the
Aguda did lose to Zionism the whole generation of young
people that I met there. The only one among us who did
remain with the Aguda was Deutschländer himself, an
uncommonly able and extraordinarily well-educated man
who after World War I set up Orthodox girls' schools for
Jews in Eastern Europe.

I remained with this group for only a little more than
six months, but this was enough for me to fall in love with
a girl for the first time. The daughter of a pious tailor from
Kalisz and thus a Russian citizen, she was a very beautiful
girl who combined flirtatiousness with piousness in a way
I did not quite understand at the time. For her sake I even
attended Sabbath afternoon services in the Alte Synagoge
where she had the women's section practically to herself,
her curls resplendent as she rocked in prayer in the first
row. The reason for my attendance was that we would
afterwards go for a walk. I wrote her school essays for her,
but when I tried to kiss her in Treptow Park a year later
she was insufferably coy, and so we parted company.
Twenty-five years later I saw her in the audience when I
gave a Hebrew lecture in Tel Aviv. Afterwards she came
up to me and said: "I am Yetka." She had become a much

sought-after English-language speaker and a star of the
Zionist women's organization (WIZO).

The Aguda, in any case, had attracted me more powerfully than the Zionist student organizations which, as I
have already mentioned, regarded us as potential new
members. In those days there were still two such groups,
and they finally merged early in 1914. Both invited us to
their inaugural drinking parties—in the fall of 1913 and
the spring of 1914 respectively. The *"Komment"* [rites]
that I got to see and hear on these occasions so outraged
me—as an example of the very kind of assimilationism
which I wanted no part of—that together with three or
four others I firmly resolved to have nothing further to do
with organizations of that ilk. I stuck to this decision,
too, and from that time on the objects of my contempt
regarded me as an eccentric sectarian and an asocial type.
A similar fate befell an attempt to recruit me for the
Jewish hiking association *Blau-Weiss* [Blue-White], which
some of my friends joined. It was a Zionist version of
the *Wandervogel,* and combined German romanticism
with the neo-Jewish kind. In fact, I did enjoy wandering
through the beautiful surroundings of Berlin, but I preferred to do so alone or in the company of Erich Brauer, a
friend from Jung Juda. (He was a graphic artist who later
became an ethnologist and wrote a standard work about
the Yemenite Jews.) I had absolutely no desire to hike
through the countryside in droves singing songs from the
Zupfgeigenhansel [the official songbook of the *Wandervogel*]
or the Jung Juda songbook, which also contained some
Zionist songs and even Hebrew and Yiddish ones. After
two so-called trial outings, I quit. My demand that young
Jews should first of all learn Hebrew was ideologically
incontestable, but it would have required more sacrifice
and effort than those students and hikers spent on their

ceremonies and nature experiences. My earliest essays, written between 1915 and 1917, reflected my rejection of the war fervor and my polemic against what then called itself the Jewish youth movement. The responses to my writings said that I undoubtedly had the courage of my convictions, but that I was totally inartistic and a purely intellectual type. Obviously there was nothing more to be said.

The author's father, Arthur Scholem (1863–1925)

The author's mother, Betty Scholem (1866–1946)

The Scholem brothers in November 1904 (*from left to right*): Reinhold Scholem, 13; Erich Scholem, 10;

Werner Scholem, 8; Gershom Scholem, 6

Gershom Scholem in Giessbach, Switzerland, 1913

Gershom Scholem in Berlin, 1917

IV

Student
in Berlin (1915–1916)

MOST OF THE members of Jung Juda, like myself, were opposed to World War I. Many of us decided in those years to go to Palestine if we survived the war.

My opposition to the war in thought and deed became known and soon led to a crisis. In February 1915 the *Jüdische Rundschau* published an article entitled *"Wir und der Krieg"* [We and the War], written in the throes of *"Bubertät"* [Buberty], a popular term for the effusive imitations of Buber by the great master's disciples. The article culminated in the following sentence: "And so we went to war—not despite our being Jews, but because of our being Zionists." This made me hit the roof. I composed a letter to the editor in which I vehemently protested against this concoction and demanded that Zionist periodicals refrain from publishing articles that glorified the war as long as the prevailing censorship prevented public expression of an opposing view. I also presented the position I and others held regarding the war. The text of this letter is preserved in the diary that I kept intermittently during those years. The protest was signed by fifteen members of our group and even by my brother Werner.

Imprudently enough, I had put this letter in my brief-case, as my friend and fellow student Edgar Blum also wished to sign it. While I was taking a walk in the school yard during recess, someone from my class ferreted out the letter and read it. He did not have time to copy it down, but it furnished enough ground to denounce me. As a consequence, the school opened an investigation. Although the director of the school, a man of sterling character, and two of my teachers opposed outright expulsion, I had to leave school in March 1915, just a year before graduation. Nevertheless, their relatively liberal treatment of the case allowed me to take the final examinations before a special committee as an external student. In October 1915 I applied to the district school committee and was referred to the Königstädtisches Realgymnasium. When I had taken the exams and was waiting for the results of the oral in the hall in front of the teachers' room, the German teacher came out and said: "There's one thing that bothers us about you. Obviously you're a gifted young man. You've passed all the tests with flying colors. [He had assigned me an essay on the subject "No Oak is Felled by the First Stroke."] But why on earth did you leave school in your last year in order to 'continue your education privately,' as your final certificate indicates?" This embarrassed me, and I hemmed and hawed. If I did not want to spoil my chances I could not very well say (much as my pride demanded it) that I had been forced to leave because I had expressed un-patriotic sentiments. So I only stared into space in embarrassment. "Oh, I understand," said the teacher, giving me a sympathetic clap on the shoulder. "Trouble with a girl, eh?" Whereupon he returned with a look of satisfaction to the teachers' room. To have seduced a girl was only a sort of gentleman's misdemeanor; thus I managed to graduate from secondary school after all.

Understandably enough, my father was very agitated about my expulsion and the reasons for it. He had had enough of me, he stated, and was going to send me to Stettin or Greifswald to be apprenticed to a *"Heringsbändiger"* [herring tamer]—Berlin slang for a grocer. My uncle Theobald and my aunt Käthe Schiepan-Hirsch interceded for me, and one of my aunt's friends who had heard about the trouble I'd been in told her about a section in the statutes of the University of Berlin that dealt with the institution of the so-called *Kleine Matrikel*. According to this regulation, anyone who could demonstrate he had completed all but a year or two of secondary school could register as a regular student for four to six semesters, though only in the liberal arts or in agriculture. Such students enjoyed all rights, but were not permitted to present themselves for examinations. This privilege had been introduced in the last century by the Prussian government, for the benefit of the sons of Prussian Junkers who had to take over their fathers' estates but were perhaps not equally well endowed with intellectual gifts. As regular students in liberal arts or agriculture, they could conceivably further their general or professional education; above all, however (and evidently this was the intent of the regulation), they could become full members of a student fraternity and acquire social polish (and contacts) there. The authorities had no intention of publicizing this regulation, which was of course formulated in general terms. True, it was spelled out in the university's statutes, but who read such things? If the existence of the *Kleine Matrikel* had become duly known, a considerable number of gifted young Jews would probably have left school at the age of sixteen, two years before graduation, rushed to the universities and easily absorbed the material of the last two years of secondary school in six to nine months. I never met another Jew who knew about this statute, let alone made use of it.

Among my non-Jewish schoolmates I only had three relationships, especially during the last two or three years of school, that could actually be called friendships. I suffered far less in school from anti-Semitic harassment than from the teasing about my jughandle ears, an inherited trait that almost all Scholems, going back three or four generations, had in common. My father at least had turned this to advantage: through long training he had acquired the ability to wiggle his ears—something that I unfortunately never managed to do. What drew me to two of my three non-Jewish school friends was a love of chess and an indefinable human empathy. Neither one shared my attitude toward the war, but they behaved in a comradely manner, and we kept in touch until they were conscripted into the army. One of them, Rudolf Ziegler, wrote me a letter fifty years later in care of my publisher, asking whether I was perhaps the Scholem whose collection of essays, *Judaica,* he had bought in a Berlin bookstore. It had reminded him of the schoolmate who had been so enthusiastic about everything Jewish, even then. I would have liked to see him again, but he died before my next visit to Berlin. About the second friend—Rudolf Korte, who later became a chemist—my older brothers, who had business dealings with him, told me that his behavior during the Nazi period had been extraordinarily decent. But the one to whom I felt closest was Erwin Briese, the son of a dental technician by the Märkischer Park. His parents literally starved themselves to pay for their son's tuition. Briese, a very broad, tall young man with rough manners but a gentle disposition, was particularly attached to me. He had a variety of interests and was the only one in this circle who shared my attitude toward the world war. During the school's proceedings against me he visited me daily to discuss everything and give me advice. He often said that he did not have a strong enough character to shirk military duty, though he was certain that he would be killed in the war. He proved to be right.

The student population at my school, by the way, was about twenty or twenty-five percent Jewish.

In the last two years before I left school I had developed a strong inclination toward mathematics, and a certain talent in the same area, and so I chose this as my major subject at the university. Our mathematics teacher Franz Goldscheider, whom I have already mentioned elsewhere, greatly encouraged me in this, while he despised philosophy, my first minor, and in his classes missed no opportunity to snipe at the fancies of the philosophers. In our conversations, he never made any allusion whatever to the events that had led to my expulsion from school—he had been among my advocates—but regularly, twice a week, he gave me the material and the specific assignments that I would have to complete for the last year of school and the final examination. He passed over my Jewish interests in silence, too, though I sometimes mentioned them almost casually (I knew that he was a baptized Jew).

I applied myself to these studies for more than four years and completed them not with the doctorate but with the *Staatsexamen* [state examination qualifying a student for a high school teacher's career, roughly equivalent to the American master's degree]. From several of my teachers, primarily Frobenius, Knopp, and Hermann Amandus Schwarz (one of Weierstrass's foremost students), I learned the meaning of mathematical elegance. I used to write out their lectures in full when I got home, and even today I could present Frobenius's four-hour introductory lecture on higher algebra on the basis of my notes. I shall never forget the first lecture given by Schwarz, who—following in the footsteps of Goldscheider, so to speak—began the term not with a definition of mathematics, but with the following sentence: "Philosophy is the systematic misuse of a terminology expressly invented for this purpose." Not until much later did I find out that this statement, which was too marvelous to be true, was not an original definition, but had been devised about twenty-five years previously. It goes without saying that mathematics fared better with such a definition. I soon realized, to be sure, that there was no dearth of philosophies of mathematics with the most antithetical tendencies—by great mathematicians and little philosophers as well as by great philosophers and little mathematicians. At any rate, I never encountered an author who was equally great in both disciplines. Bertrand Russell remained a borderline case throughout his life.

Despite my great interest in mathematics I was aware of the fact that my forte did not lie in that field. This became overwhelmingly clear to me in my fifth semester—in the summer of 1917—when I participated in an algebra seminar with the newly appointed professors Erhard Schmidt and Issai Schur, both important mathematicians. Whenever a problem appeared that stumped us and gave even the professors trouble, one of the professors would turn to a very ordinary-looking young man who sat in one of the top rows of the amphitheater in which the seminar was held and say: "Well, Herr Siegel, what do you say to that?" Herr Siegel almost always had a solution. I saw what a first-rate mathematician is and how a true mathematical mind works. The presence of Carl Ludwig Siegel, later one of the greatest mathematicians of my generation, was a signal to me that I would never achieve what could be expected of an authentic mathematician.

Yet I stuck with the study of mathematics and physics, because I hoped that I might find a position as a mathematics teacher at a Hebrew-language school in Palestine.

I supplemented my studies of those years by acquiring a considerable mathematical library. Number theory, algebra, and function theory were particularly to my liking. Thus two souls dwelled, alas, in my breast at that time.

My father was not pleased about these inclinations. Even in my presence he was fond of complaining: "My son the gentleman engages in nothing but unprofitable pursuits. My son the gentleman is interested in mathematics, pure mathematics. I ask my son the gentleman: What do you want? As a Jew you have no chance of a university career. You cannot get an important position. Take up engineering, go to a technical college, then you can do as much math in your free time as you like. But no, my son the gentleman does not want to become an engineer, he wants only pure mathematics. My son the gentleman is interested in *Yiddishkeit.* So I say to my son the gentleman: All right, become a rabbi, then you can have all the *Yiddishkeit* you want. No, my son the gentleman won't hear of becoming a rabbi. Unprofitable pursuits." This was my father's position. He died in 1925, just a few months before I received a university appointment in Jerusalem for these unprofitable Jewish pursuits.

All the different inclinations that I have described above naturally led me to philosophical interests and reflections at an early age. *"Der kleine Schwegler,"* as the brief history of philosophy published by Reclam was called, and Wilhelm Wundt's *Einleitung in die Philosophie* [Introduction to Philosophy] were the first writings that I encountered in my last year at secondary school. I did not understand Kant as yet, but a number of Schleiermacher's translations of Platonic dialogues moved me. I began to regret that I did not know Greek, a gap that I did not fill until 1919–20, when I studied in Munich. While I did find a few distinguished teachers in mathematics, there was no one of the same eminence in philosophy. The philosophy professors at the University of Berlin left me cold. I must confess that I was particularly annoyed at one of Ernst Cassirer's lectures on the pre-Socratics, because he stopped whenever it seemed to get interesting and said: "But this would take us too far afield." Adolf Lasson, the "last Hegelian" at the university, who had been my father's homeroom teacher at the Luisenstädtisches Real-Gymnasium forty years earlier, at the age of eighty-three gave a public lecture about Hegel which was uncommonly lively from a rhetorical point of view, but unconvincing. He still had a large audience, but there were only a handful of people at the lectures of the astronomer Wilhelm Förster, who was the same age. Förster was the founder of the *Gesellschaft für ethische Kultur* [Ethical Culture Society], the philosophic predecessor of monism. This particular course of lectures, on Johannes Kepler, was perhaps the most impressive I heard at that institution because of the ethos and, if I may say so, the profound piousness of this atheist. But in any case, that is where I began to learn to read Kant.

One semester before I went to the university, Georg Simmel, its most eminent teacher of philosophy, had accepted an appointment at the University of Strassburg. Despite his great reputation, in the course of thirty years he had been unable to obtain a full professorship in Germany, for, as he wrote in a letter that later became famous, *"hebraeus sum"* [I am a Jew]. Here was a man whose parents had left the Jewish fold before 1850, who was totally estranged from everything Jewish and yet was widely regarded as the very quintessence of a Talmudist.

When the University of Heidelberg once put his name at
the head of a list of candidates for a professorship, an
influential Berlin historian urged the wife of the Grand
Duke of Baden (a man regarded as liberal) to make sure
that the prestigious Heidelberg chair was not disgraced
by such an out-and-out Jewish spirit. Buber was a disciple
and great admirer of Simmel, and he sometimes pointed
out to Simmel that a man like himself ought to be interested in seeing to it that men of his type did not disappear.
This did not elicit a response from Simmel, although he,
like everyone else, must have noticed that the productive
spirits who responded to his intellectuality were almost
exclusively Jews. Much later Buber told me that in all the
years in which he associated with Simmel he had heard
him say "we" in connection with the Jews only once (and
that to Buber's considerable surprise). That was when
Simmel had read Buber's first book on Hasidism, *The
Tales of Rabbi Nachman,* and said slowly and thoughtfully:
"We certainly are a very strange people."

But I did hear in Berlin a great philosopher who was
both a great man and a major Jewish figure: Hermann
Cohen, the head of the Marburg school of neo-Kantianism.
I did not attend the lectures on the philosophy of religion
which he gave—in his seventies—at the Lehranstalt (later
Hochschule) für die Wissenschaft des Judentums on
Artilleriestrasse, but I did hear a few of his talks on themes
from his work-in-progress, *Die Religion der Vernunft aus
den Quellen des Judentums* [The Religion of Reason from
Jewish Sources]. These were given as part of the institution's well-attended public "Monday lectures." Whether
one agreed with Cohen's views or not, he was an awe-
inspiring figure. By conventional standards he was quite
ugly: unusually short and with a disproportionately large
head. Seeing him taught me for the first time what beauty
can be contained in an ugly head. As an old man he spoke

in a high-pitched, emotional voice. Actually, only his
forehead protruded from the speaker's lectern. But from
time to time, when he uttered certain words relating to
good or evil, such as *prophetism* or *pantheism* (the particular object of his hatred), his enormous head would suddenly appear above the lectern for the duration of a sentence, radiating with passion. It was a memorable sight.

Cohen was the author of the most profound statement
that an opponent of Zionism ever made about the movement. One day in 1914 he turned to Franz Rosenzweig,
whom he reproached with having too tolerant an attitude
toward Zionism, and (according to Rosenzweig's written
account) lowered his voice to a thunderous stage whisper:
"Die Kerle wollen glücklich sein!" [Those fellows want to be
happy!] I knew many of Cohen's pupils. In his old age he
was considered a truly biblical figure by everyone, including his adversaries. His last student was my friend Harry
(Aharon) Heller from Jung Juda who took Cohen's tutorial on Maimonides in the winter semester of 1917/18, at
the end of which Cohen died.

If I had to struggle with any inner conflict, it was the
conflict between my mathematical and my Jewish souls.
Yet the direction of my life was clearly determined in
those early years, particularly from 1916 on, since I had
resolved to tie my future to the building of a new Jewish
life in Eretz Yisrael. For me Zion was a symbol that linked
our origin and our utopian goal in a religious rather than a
geographical sense. I regarded my next years primarily as
years of apprenticeship in preparation for my life there,
and since the problematic nature of the Jewish situation
in Germany had begun to assume ever clearer outlines in
my mind, I did not try to sink roots in that country.

In 1913 I decided to read through the Hebrew Bible
from the beginning. If memory serves, this first reading

took about four years. I did not keep the four volumes of
the Letteris edition but replaced them as soon as I could
with a supposedly more scholarly one, though today I am
no longer certain whether it was not a step backward
disguised as progress. Sixty years later, when I visited
Friedrich Dürrenmatt, I was fascinated by his father's
Bible, which Dürrenmatt keeps in his Neuchâtel home.
In it the clergyman had entered the dates of his six
readings of the complete Hebrew Bible.

This was how things stood with me when in July 1915,
toward the end of my first semester, I met Walter Benjamin. Since I have written an entire book about my
relationship with him,* I shall not deal with it here. But I
do want to say something about the significance that this
friendship—the most important of my life—has had for
me. Surely my passionate attachment to things Jewish
played a central part in the development of our friendship. Paradoxical though it may seem in light of his nearly
total ignorance in Jewish matters, Benjamin never ques-
tioned this attachment but, if anything, encouraged it.
When I met him, despite all his metaphysical openness he
was living almost without direction. He had only one
guiding star, as I was soon able to recognize: the late
Friedrich Hölderlin, whose work I first discovered through
Benjamin. Philosophical and literary interests brought us
together, but the questions he put to me in his wholly
original and unexpected formulations when I spoke of
Jewish matters were extraordinarily stimulating to me and
forced me to concentrate much more intensively than I
was called upon to do in the circle of my young Zionist
friends. My closest friends from Jung Juda—Harry Heymann (who died on the front in 1918), Walter Czapski,

*Walter Benjamin—The Story of a Friendship (Philadelphia: Jewish Publi-
cation Society, 1981).

Aharon Heller, Shlomo Krolik, Karl Türkischer, and Erich Brauer—saw eye to eye with me in their Zionist convictions and decisions (if not in other ways) to such an extent that we simply confirmed one another's positions and only seldom discussed basic questions. Our stand on the war was in those days an emotional bond, the strength of which could not be overestimated. Every one of us went to Eretz Yisrael sooner or later. Heller virtually radiated integrity and was very intelligent; for some years his integrity seemed exemplary to me. Many years later he became one of the leading physicians of Israel, but the bond between us had given way to an uncanny and unresolvable estrangement. Together with Brauer I issued in 1915 and 1916 three numbers of a lithographed periodical which was produced in our printshop (without my father's knowledge) and bore the symbolic title *Die blauweisse Brille* [The Blue-White Eyeglasses]. It was circulated in a limited Zionist circle. We wrote this periodical ourselves to combat the confusion reigning in less radical Zionist circles. Benjamin was simply of a different caliber. In 1915, during the visits I had made with my brother Werner to the Hasenheide, I had for the first time met a poet in the person of Helmut Schönlank, the son of a well-known Social Democratic leader in Leipzig and grandson of a rabbi. In Benjamin I met for the first time a man with an utterly original mind, one that immediately appealed to me and moved me. Thus we probably contributed our share to each other's development, and I would say that I owe him at least as much—on an entirely different plane—as he owed to me.

It was the *Blauweisse Brille* that brought me into direct contact with Martin Buber. In March 1916 we had published a biting caricature and parody of him (if "published" was the word for the manner in which our 50 copies were distributed). Buber reacted in a surprising way: he invited us to visit him. I had been very irritated by his attitude in wartime, particularly by an essay entitled *"Kinesis,"* which had appeared in the *Neue Merkur,* a rather good, short-lived monthly. Nor had I forgotten the article by his disciple Heinrich Margulies (who had long since defected and joined an opposing party that supported political Zionism), an article that had caused me to be kicked upstairs, and now I somewhat petulantly reproached Buber with it. At that time Buber was exactly twice my age. He behaved magnificently and listened seriously to my speeches (while Brauer, who was very shy, kept silent) and not without indicating that he had changed his position. As a person he made a great impression upon me, and my further meetings with him, which soon followed, reinforced this impression. He also told us of a periodical which he was editing and which was about to appear: *Der Jude* [The Jew], a name that sixty years ago betrayed more than a little pride to Jewish and Christian ears alike. In choosing this name, Buber was reviving the title of a periodical that had achieved fame eighty years before, during the struggle for the emancipation of the Jews. But while Gabriel Riesser and his authors fought for the emancipation of the Jews as Germans, Buber's *Der Jude,* surely the best Jewish journal in the German language that ever existed, fought for the emancipation of the Jews as Jews, a people among peoples. Buber invited me to become a contributor, and some of my early writings are included throughout its volumes, among them my first essays on the Kabbala and a number of translations of Hebrew poetry and prose. Even though I later had great and far-reaching differences of opinion with Buber, I always greatly respected him—even revered him—as a person. I often met with him in the years before my emigration, and he followed my career very attentively. I

could not be blind to his weaknesses, but my memories of
the many conversations about Hasidism and the Kabbala
which I had with him when I turned to the study of the
original sources, as well as the expectations he evidently
had for me, provided a counterbalance to Walter Benjamin's largely negative evaluation of him.

A great deal happened during these war years, particularly 1916 and 1917, during which time I got around
quite a bit. My studies and my Zionist activities brought
me together with new people from very different circles.
For an extended period in the summer of 1916 I left
Berlin and went to Heidelberg and Oberstdorf in the
Allgäu—because our family doctor, my father's youngest
brother, claimed I was a "neurasthenic," or prone to "bad
nerves." This diagnosis seemed to reflect a well-known
Berlin saying of that time: *"Haste nie und raste nie, dann
haste nie Neurasthenie"* [Never hurry and never rest, and
with no neurasthenia you'll be blessed]. Perhaps the doctor was also influenced by the fact that my military service
had been deferred twice.

At the University of Berlin, I attended a major lecture
course given by the newly appointed Ernst Troeltsch.
Troeltsch had transferred from the School of Theology
to the School of Liberal Arts, but introduced himself with
a course on the philosophy of religion, a subject that
vitally interested me. There I happened to sit next to a
lady about thirty-five years of age. What attracted my
attention was not so much her striking dark beauty and
bearing as the notes—protesting against Troeltsch's somewhat too "cultivated" presentation—that she dashed off
in a large passionate script, using an enormous number of
exclamation points and question marks. The expression
on her face reflected her emotions as effectively as the
expressionistic explosions in her notebook, which I could

not keep from peering at over her shoulder. Thus we struck up a conversation. She was Grete Lissauer, the wife of an associate professor of medicine at the University of Königsberg who was on military duty. The following summer I spent a great deal of time in Heidelberg with that lady; she was an ardent pacifist and a sharp-witted feminist. Grete introduced me to some Jewish female students who were from completely assimilated families, some of them baptized, and had now discovered their Jewish hearts without quite knowing what to do with them. There was Toni Halle (whose father was one of the very few unbaptized higher judges in Prussia), a Germanist close to the completion of her studies and a girl who was beginning to feel uneasy about the cause of Jewish assimilation. She was participating in a seminar given by Karl Jaspers, who liked to gather information about the most remote intellectual phenomena in preparation for his book *Psychologie der Weltanschauungen*. I asked her what she was doing in that seminar. "I am writing a paper on Hasidism." With somewhat feigned naiveté I went on questioning her: "What do you know about it?" "What I have read in Buber's books, of course." "Is that all?" "Well, what else is there?" This is how our friendship began. I induced her to take up Hebrew; she went to Eretz Yisrael only a few years after me, and although her Hebrew remained rather wretched, she became one of the most respected and most influential teachers in the country and the founder of a very progressive secondary school. It was a similar story with Käthe Holländer, about whom Grete Lissauer told me: "Look at her, she is a born Bedouin—the European clothes she's wearing are all wrong on her." She was from a baptized family in Naumburg, and not long before I met her she had returned to Judaism, to the great displeasure of her parents. She studied mathematics and then went to Lithuania as a teacher in a Jewish high school. There she married a Hebrew poet, and she too later came to Israel. From the stories told by these and other students who came from the milieus in which assimilation had already gone to the limit and even beyond, I learned a great deal that helped me understand the situation of the Jews in Germany. A third student whom I met at Grete Lissauer's home represented a different type. Valeria Grünwald, a medical student from Erfurt, had parents who had come from Hungary and who tried to compensate for their two daughters' rebellion through German superpatriotism. These were my first Hebrew students. Grete Lissauer herself drifted between the highest ideals of humanity and strong feelings of Jewish pride. During the entire time that I knew her she was working on a drama written in iambic pentameters, called *Aspasia;* for she wanted to portray through this classical figure her own ideal and its tensions. On many evenings she read to me and other friends from it, and afterwards we took long walks by the Schlossberg. In her home I met for the first time a Jew who had become a Catholic out of conviction, but I did not know that while I had personal contact with him. Thus I read with great interest Max Fischer's first book which had just appeared, *Heinrich Heine der deutsche Jude* [Heinrich Heine, the German Jew]. I viewed it as the analysis of a German who had seriously reflected on the Jews in general and the figure of Heine in particular, and I marveled at the insight that a German displayed here in criticism as well. Three days before my departure from Heidelberg, Fischer revealed to me that he was an apostate and had written his book from the standpoint of a Jewish convert. Grete Lissauer died in Moscow in the middle 1920s as a believing Communist.

From Heidelberg I made a number of visits to Buber, who had just moved to Heppenheim, and I conferred with him about the first issues of *Der Jude,* to which I had many objections, and about my own collaboration. Once I incurred the anger of Buber and his wife, who was otherwise well disposed toward me (and remained so), when over coffee I made a flippant, deprecatory remark about Georg Simmel, who was highly regarded in the Buber house. On another of those visits, Buber told me that following deliberations in which he had participated, a number of young men and women from Berlin with strong Jewish and social interests had decided to establish a *"Jüdisches Volksheim"* [Jewish community center]. It was going to be opened in the course of the summer in the so-called Scheunenviertel on the Alexanderplatz, on Grenadierstrasse, a neighborhood that housed many refugee families from the eastern war zones. He described the initiators as Zionists who had been influenced by the ideas of the Russian *Narodnaya Volya* [The National Will Party, the terrorist arm of the Populist movement, organized in 1879] about "going among the people," and they wanted to take up work in that district where poverty and prostitution were facts of life. From this work they expected mutual assistance and inspiration. Buber told me that it might be important for me to participate, and suggested that I take a closer look at it after my return to Berlin. The leader was Siegfried Lehmann, a young doctor who was very well known among Jewish students as a so-called "cultural Zionist" (in contrast to political Zionism). Lehmann had maintained close contact with the social reform-minded wing of the *"Freie Studentenschaft"* [Free Students' Association]. Under the leadership of Ernst Joël, this wing pursued similar goals and maintained a settlement house in a Charlottenburg workers' district. The discussion with Kurt Hiller to which I owe my

acquaintance with Walter Benjamin took place there. (I
have described that evening in my book about Benjamin.)

   In the evening the Jewish children from Eastern Europe
who were the female volunteers' primary objects of care
were of course not in evidence, for they were home with
their parents. But the male and female volunteers would
meet there evenings with friends of the cause for discussion and lectures. The friends of the cause were primarily
members of the Russian-Jewish intelligentsia—some very
impressive figures among them—who were studying or
working in Berlin. The Volksheim people were almost
exclusively Western Jews, more or less Zionistically
oriented, who had only a very rudimentary knowledge of
Jewish affairs but were utterly devoted to their work even
though they did not yet fully understand what it would
imply. Within the framework of that cult of the Eastern
Jews that I have already mentioned, the Jewish socialists
from Russia, most of them highly educated people, were
highly respected as potential advisers. These exiles, whose
most outstanding members I knew quite well, enjoyed
fulfilling their function, not least because many of the
girls were extremely charming, even beautiful. The indis-
putable central figure in this circle was a most impressive
person who was already in her late twenties. That was
Fräulein Gertrude Welkanoz, known simply as Gertrude,
a young lady with a completely natural dignity and a
unique authority. Though she worked in a bank, she
seemed to be the only person in the group with some
understanding of social work; but that was nothing com-
pared to the near-magical influence that she exerted on
all those girls. I regard it as one of the great losses to the
building of Israel that because of her personal circumstances—she married a decided non-Zionist, the secondhand book dealer Ernst Weil—this extraordinary woman
never came to settle in Eretz Yisrael.

When I arrived at the Volksheim for the first time, my eyes encountered a strange scene. The volunteers and visitors were sitting on chairs; on the floor, picturesquely grouped around Gertrude, their skirts draped aesthetically, sat the young girls, including (as we now know) Felice Bauer, Franz Kafka's fiancée. Siegfried Lehmann was reading from the poetry of Franz Werfel, and in my mind's ear I can still hear the *"Gespräch an der Mauer des Paradieses"* [Conversation at the Paradise Wall]. But I was shocked: what surrounded me was an atmosphere of aesthetic ecstasy—probably the last thing I had come there to find. At the end of the evening it was announced that Lehmann would soon give a talk on "The Problem of Jewish Religious Education." I was as curious as I was skeptical about what he would have to say on that subject. In the meantime I went there once more, and again I disliked the atmosphere as well as a seriously intended discussion concerning a question that seemed more like a joke to me: whether it would be all right to hang in the rooms of the Volksheim a reproduction of a famous portrait of the Virgin Mary. And this at a center where the children of poor but strictly Orthodox Jewish families from Eastern Europe were to spend the day until they were picked up by their parents in the afternoon! Among those present was Dr. Jacob Grommer, a first-rate mathematician about thirty-five years old who a few years previously had contracted acromegaly. The disease had given him a grotesquely distorted square face with a very grave expression and made him virtually unable to speak intelligibly. An unusually tall man, he had been a Talmudic wunderkind in his youth before turning to mathematics, a field in which great things were expected of him. His disease, which was now in remission, had thrown him largely on his own resources, but something drew him to the Volksheim, where his profound Jewish knowledge was respected. A few sentences from him, spoken in a rough, barely intelligible voice, put an end to the ghastly discussion about the painting.

I went to hear Lehmann's lecture, and it aroused particularly vehement objections on my part because I sensed in it the lack of seriousness which expressed itself in the group's interpretations of Buber's interpretations of Hasidism without their knowing anything about historical Judaism (as I formulated it in my diary of that time). One week later a very heated discussion of this lecture, principally between Lehmann and myself, took place. To Lehmann's understandable annoyance I demanded that people learn Hebrew and go to the sources instead of occupying themselves with such literary twaddle. This discussion led to an angry exchange of letters between Lehmann and myself as well as to my break with the Volksheim. I have preserved this correspondence; Walter Benjamin planned to publish it in his projected periodical *Angelus Novus* in 1923. What I could not have known was that Kafka's fiancée informed Kafka about Lehmann's lecture and the ensuing passionate debate. How shall I describe my astonishment when fifty years later Kafka's letters to Felice Bauer were published and I read there that Kafka decidedly took my side: "The discussion you describe is typical; theoretically I am always inclined to favor proposals such as those made by Herr Scholem, which demand the utmost and by so doing achieve nothing. So one simply mustn't appraise such proposals and their value by the actual result laid before one. Incidentally, I think this is generally applicable. Actually, Scholem's proposals in themselves are not impracticable."* (It took an ironic protest to the publisher to rectify the identification of my name as that of Sholom Aleichem, the somewhat more

*Letters to Felice (New York: Schocken Books, 1973), p. 505.

famous Yiddish classic who was already dead at that time.) Lehmann later reaped much credit for his social work in Kovno and in Israel, where he founded the children's village Ben Shemen and administered it until his death. As a theoretician of Jewish education, however, he remained unclear to the end, being still preoccupied with the old Buberian "religiosity" without religion.

Not long after Kafka had written that letter, I read his legend "Before the Law" in the *Almanach der Neuen Jugend . . . auf 1917.* It made a tremendous impression upon me and many of my generation and prompted me to keep track, as far as possible, of the few writings of Kafka that were published before his death. In modern literature, at any rate, the works of Kafka have meant more to me than any other.

That autumn I met, through Walter Benjamin, another remarkable person with whom I associated a great deal until my emigration and to whom I also imparted an elementary knowledge of Hebrew. This was Erich Gutkind (1877–1965). Even when he was very old, every time I came to New York, where he had found refuge from Hitler, I paid a visit to his indescribably shabby rooms on an upper floor of the Master Hotel on Riverside Drive. Gutkind was the son of one of the wealthiest Berlin Jews, whose villa, in which Gutkind's mother lived up to her death, stood opposite that of the Rathenau family. For reasons never quite clear to me, Gutkind no longer shared in this wealth when I met him. He was an altogether mystically attuned soul who had delved into virtually all fields of learning in order to find their secret center, and yet he had had no contact with anything Jewish and had been almost on the verge of converting to Catholicism. A few years before the war he had published a mystical treatise entitled *Siderische Geburt* [Sidereal

Birth] which gives clear evidence of his quest. The reception of this work showed that he was not alone in the attempt to integrate modern science into a mystic dimension. He was a man of superlatives, even in conversation, and his rapturous mode of expression, which in conversation was strangely mixed with Berlin slang, deprived his writing of a great deal of the clarity that would have been required there. He was probably the least-known member of the Forte Circle, that small group of men—Frederik van Eeden, Buber, Walther Rathenau, Theodor Däubler, Paul Bjerre, Florens Christian Rang, and three or four others—who in 1913/14 conceived an idea which would seem almost incredible if it had not been confirmed for me, and in almost identical language, by such dissimilar men as Buber and Gutkind: a small group of people would set up a community devoted to intellectual and spiritual activity for a certain period of time to engage without any reservations in a creative exchange of ideas; in doing so they might manage to shake the world off its hinges (to put it esoterically but clearly). Gutkind showed me the voluminous correspondence among the projected participants and claimed that the underlying design had not been frustrated by the outbreak of the First World War which had canceled the projected decisive meeting at Forte dei Marmi (as is stated in the literature today) but had essentially collapsed in April 1914, during a week the men spent together at Potsdam. Gutkind told strange things about this circle of anarchistic aristocrats of the spirit and the days at Potsdam in which he participated.

When I met Gutkind and his wife Lucie in the fall of 1916, he had rediscovered his Jewishness, or rather, an overwhelming feeling of belonging made him want to delve into this world, which had hitherto been closed to him. He lived in Nowawes near Potsdam, and I visited him on a number of occasions and taught him Hebrew for a few months. I soon realized that he was not up to the demands that he himself made and that he would get bogged down in mystical rhetoric, but I liked him very much as a human being (though I liked his wife less). We established a relationship of great trust. From our first conversation to his very last years he struggled intensively with the problem of religious ritual, the subject of many discussions between us. It was a question that did not interest Benjamin, for example, while it became more and more central for Gutkind and toward the end of his life almost led him into the camp of the Lubavitch Hasidim in Brooklyn. To my great surprise he became the director of the Jüdisches Volksheim shortly after World War I (I was in Switzerland at the time), but soon there was a rebellion against him by the staff, who did not want to listen to his talk about the need for ritual in their work as well. He was a close friend of Florens Christian Rang who was akin to him in many respects, primarily in his basic gnostic attitude, though Rang was intellectually vastly superior. It was Gutkind who brought Rang and Walter Benjamin together; later they became close friends. In Gutkind's library I became acquainted with many remarkable mystical writings, though I could not say that I read them all. But my philosophical education was truly enriched by that library—through Gottlob B. Jäsche's multivolume, 150-year-old work on philosophical pantheism, a work that is not at all without merit but was already virtually forgotten in my time.

V

Pension Struck (1917)

A GREAT CRISIS developed between my father and myself
at the beginning of the year 1917. My brother Werner
had been wounded in the foot in the Serbian campaign
of 1916 and spent a rather long time in the military
hospital at Halle an der Saale. He had almost recovered,
though he still had a slight limp, and he used the opportunity to establish contact with like-minded people in
that city, which had a very strong Social Democratic
antiwar minority. On January 27, the Kaiser's birthday
and an official holiday, he took part in an antiwar demonstration of the extreme left and was arrested. He was
charged with *Landesverrat* [treason]—(he had appeared
in his uniform!)—though later the charge was changed to
Majestätsbeleidigung [lese-majesty]. He got word to me
through a confidant two days later. When I heard that he
was in prison for treason, I immediately realized that the
news would act like a bombshell in our house. I took all
my papers, especially my diaries, and brought them to my
friend Heller. Two days later my father received official

notification from the authorities that his son had been arrested and would be court-martialed for treason. A terrible scene ensued at the dinner table. When I raised a mild objection to one of my father's assertions, he flew into a rage and said he had now had enough of the two of us, that Social Democracy and Zionism were all the same, anti-German activities which he would no longer tolerate in his house, and that he never wanted to see me again. The following day I received a registered letter from him in which he demanded that I leave his house on the first of March and henceforth shift for myself. He said that he declined to have any further dealings with me, and that since I was going on twenty he was no longer obliged to support me. He was going to pay me a hundred marks on March 1, and that would be that.

There was a great uproar. I was determined to accept the ouster and not go along with any attempts at mediation that might be made. All this quickly became known in Jung Juda and at the office of the *Jüdische Rundschau*. The editor-in-chief of the journal at that time was Dr. Max Mayer, a Bavarian Jew whose views largely coincided with mine and who was also one of the few Zionists in Germany who had really delved into Hebrew. But most importantly, in this manner the news reached my friend Zalman Rubashov, about whom I shall have more to say later. He said: "A martyr of Zionism! Something will have to be done!" He arranged to meet with me: "Don't worry; you must move to the boarding house where I live. I'll see to it that you get an especially low rate and a good room." Of course that was fine with me.

It was in this manner that I moved to Pension Struck at the Wilmersdorf end of Uhlandstrasse. I lived there until I was inducted into the army; it was the only period of time I ever spent in the west end of Berlin. What a curious place it was! The landlady, a distant relative

of the artist Hermann Struck, kept a strictly kosher house
for a clientele of East European Jews who had long since
ceased to care about the observance of the dietary laws.
The boarders consisted predominantly of those Russian-
Jewish intellectuals with whom I was already personally
acquainted from Jung Juda or the Jüdisches Volksheim.
A young girl from a pious South German community and
I were the only German Jews there. At the table one
heard a mixture of Yiddish, Hebrew, and German with a
Russian accent. Several of the guests were adherents of
the socialist-Zionist party Poale Zion which had built its
Zionism on a Marxist foundation. The atmosphere was a
purely Zionist one, but since there already were very
different currents among the Zionists—proponents and
opponents of Yiddish, for example—there was no lack of
animated political and intellectual arguments. This made
for a highly stimulating group. As the only "real" Berliner
I was treated very amicably, though people eyed me as
one would a multicolored dog. By that time there was
already a great food shortage (it was the end of the
infamous rutabaga winter), but Frau Struck was a Jewish
widow who knew how to economize. From time to time
the pantry housed a cake which fulfilled its function late
at night, for quite a few members of this group loved
nocturnal discussions which often dragged on till two in
the morning.

The living center of Pension Struck was twenty-seven-
year-old Zalman Rubashoff (or Rubashov), who later
became president of Israel as Zalman Shazar. Rubashov,
from whom Arthur Koestler derived the name of the
hero of his novel *Darkness at Noon* (about the Moscow
trials), came from a highly respected Hasidic family in
Russia which, however, was already flirting with the
Haskalah [Enlightenment]. At the age of sixteen he was

already the wunderkind of Poale Zion. His great passion was everything Jewish, but above all Jewish history. He had come to Germany in 1912 to be trained as a historian by Friedrich Meinecke at the University of Freiburg. When the war broke out, he was interned as an enemy alien, but like many other Russian Jews he was released as early as 1915 after the Jewish organizations in Germany had rightly convinced the German government that these Russian Jews were far greater opponents of the Russian regime than of Germany—that they were, in fact, decidedly Germanophile. Thus Rubashov went to Berlin, where he only had to report to the police twice a week, and since he was fluent in Hebrew, Yiddish, and Russian, he became the specialist in all Jewish affairs for the *Jüdische Rundschau*. In addition he became very much in demand as a speaker before Zionist youth groups and the Jüdischer Arbeiterbildungsverein Peretz [Peretz Educational Association of Jewish Workers] which had its home in the Jüdisches Volksheim and represented a truce between Zionist and anti-Zionist working men from Eastern Europe for the duration of the war.

Rubashov was a spellbinding, often ecstatic speaker, one without equal. He would start quite softly, only to fall suddenly into a kind of trance after two or three minutes, a trance in which he finished his speech with great vocal power, gestures that were almost more expressive than his words, and a dramatic outpouring of sentences—even if it took an hour or two. Afterwards he would be completely exhausted and recuperated in a café or in the kitchen of Pension Struck in conversations that slowly gathered momentum.

He was phenomenal. We had never heard anything like it, and the most remarkable thing of all was that he really had something to say. There was substance to his speeches, whether he spoke about the history of Bible criticism or some aspect of Jewish history, particularly the Jewish labor movement, about Hebrew or Yiddish poets and prose writers, or about the tasks we would face in building a new society in Palestine after the war. I heard him give lectures in three languages—German, Yiddish, and Hebrew—and it was astonishing every time. He made an overwhelming impression in Germany, but to tell the truth, in Eretz Yisrael his rhetorical style, which was certainly not playacting, was not effective. Many Jews who had come from Eastern Europe could not stand that sort of thing. Perhaps they had already heard similar speakers in their countries of origin and were more allergic than partial to such oratory, even if it resounded in superb Hebrew.

By this time we were living in adjoining rooms on the lower floor of Pension Struck. Rubashov did not function before eleven in the morning. He went to bed late, read or wrote poetry, and did not appear at the office of the *Jüdische Rundschau* until about noon. But at the noonday meal or in the evening he would start to bloom. No sooner was it decided that I would move into Pension Struck than he worried about how I would manage. He came to me and said: "We have the solution! We've just received a copy of a book that recently appeared in New York. It is the second, revised edition of a book commemorating those who fell in Palestine before the war while keeping watch over the Jewish settlements; they were all members of the Zionist workers' movement. [A much smaller version of that book had already appeared in a Hebrew edition at Jaffa in 1914]. A few comrades who were expelled by the Turks in 1915 because they did not want to become Ottoman citizens have published an expanded Yiddish edition in New York. You are the man who must translate it into German! Buber is going to write the foreword [Buber used the term *Geleitwort,* 'accompanying words']. We already have a publisher, and Dr. Aron Eliasberg will pay you enough to live on for a few months." The editing of this volume, which I still own, was in the hands of two labor leaders who were completely unknown outside the Poale Zion party, David Ben-Gurion and Yitzhak Ben-Zvi. For variety's sake they used various pseudonyms for several essays. I asked Rubashov: "But how am I going to translate from Yiddish?" "But you just took Alexander Eliasberg [Aron's cousin] apart in the *Jüdische Rundschau* because of his rotten translation from the Yiddish!" "That's different." "Nonsense, you know Hebrew, I know that, so you can translate the essays originally written in Hebrew from that language; I have the original edition. That you know German you don't have to prove to me. You learned Middle High German in secondary school; surely you didn't recite Walther von der Vogelweide the other day for nothing. And the Slavic words you'll simply ask me; that's why we live next door to each other. So there you have your Yiddish." Thus I spent three hours a day for almost three months on this work, my first publication in book form which appeared anonymously in 1918: *Jiskor—ein Buch des Gedenkens an gefallene Wächter und Arbeiter im Lande Israel. Deutsche Ausgabe* [Yizkor—A Memorial Volume for Fallen Watchmen and Workers in Eretz Yisrael. German Edition]. (*Yizkor*—May He [that is, God] remember—is the first word of the prayers said at memorial services for the deceased in synagogues.) I said that my translation appeared anonymously. I was still very young and passionate, and probably a bit foolish. When some rather militaristic-sounding sentences in a number of the contributions greatly annoyed me, I wrote Buber that I could not find it in my conscience to let such things be published with my name as translator. There was some excitement, because Buber claimed that people would then regard *him* as the translator. This problem was easily solved by my signing the translation *N.N.* [*nomen nescio,* Latin for "I do not know the name," i.e., "Anon."] The book contained some magnificent essays, particularly by Joseph Chaim Brenner, one of the most important figures of Russian Jewry and the Jewish labor movement in Eretz Yisrael. (He was murdered by Arabs during the riots of May 1921.) But there was also a lot of sentimental stuff which had a great effect on the tear ducts of many male and female readers, for the book had numerous readers in both its German and Polish editions. On his eighty-fifth birthday David Ben-Gurion was astonished to hear from me that I had been his first German translator.

Before the appearance of the *Yizkor* volume there was an incident. Victor Jacobsohn, who was on the five-member Zionist executive committee and served as liaison between London and Berlin in Copenhagen, heard about the plans for publication and went to see Rubashov. He said that the book could not appear, for it would get us into great political trouble with the Turkish authorities, who could not read Yiddish but would quickly find out about a German edition. Besides, the book was too gory in places (an opinion which I shared). The discussion went back and forth fruitlessly, and then they agreed to bring the matter before Buber, who had considerable Zionist authority in those days. When the two men had presented their arguments for and against publication, Buber got up, looked heavenward, and said simply: "I have a mission." The book was published.

Rubashov was a Marxist Zionist, but he was on good terms with God even then. He felt that only when religion could no longer be used as a means for the suppression and exploitation of the masses would it fulfill its true mission in a liberated society. Stirred by some of his lectures and courses, many people expected him to pave the way to a new understanding of the messianic movements in Judaism. When my own research drew me to this area over a period of many years, I waited for a long time to see whether he would fulfill the hopes placed in him before I began to publish my own comprehensive writings on the subject. But his political ambitions stood in the way of his scholarly ones and kept him from developing his abilities fully. He wrote a number of beautiful, even stirring, essays about events and personalities of Jewish history, particularly the labor movement. Yet he wrote as a socialist romantic rather than as a scholar.

In May 1917 I received orders to report for induction on June 18; in March I had been given a physical examination and classified as *k.v.*, that is, *kriegsverwendungsfähig* [fit for active duty] in the infantry. Even though he must have found it hard to get up at five in the morning, Rubashov insisted on accompanying me to the barracks on General-Pape-Strasse. At the gate he embraced me Russian style and kissed me on both cheeks. He pressed a little black object into my hand and gazed after me wistfully as I walked away. What he had given me was a miniature edition of the Hebrew text of the Psalms in which he had inscribed the verse "May God protect you from all evil, may He protect your soul." Ever since that day, this tiny black book has accompanied me on all my peregrinations. Fifty years later, after a lifelong relationship, the two of us were neighbors again on the same street in Jerusalem, and at the end of our very dissimilar "careers" we fulfilled neighborly and not so dissimilar public functions that we had never dreamt of in Pension Struck in Berlin—Rubashov as the third president of the state of Israel and I as the third president of the Israel Academy of Sciences.

In those months before my military period I also met the great Hebrew writer S. J. Agnon, to whom close bonds of friendship bound me until his death. I had often seen him in the reading room of the library of the Jewish Community Council where he tirelessly leafed through the Hebrew card catalogue. Later I asked him what he had so intensively searched for there. "Books that I have not read yet," he replied with a guileless and yet ironic gleam in his eyes. As a young man he was of medium height, thin to the point of emaciation, with sharp features. Later, around the time of our personal acquaintance, he had to gain a lot of weight after some kidney trouble, and his figure became more rounded. I met him at the house of his first German translator, who I felt to be a very memorable and likable figure. This was Max Strauss, the brother of the poet Ludwig Strauss, an uncommonly gifted, very sensitive, and magnificent-looking young lawyer still in his twenties. I believe his magnificent appearance was his ruin, for he had too easy a time of it everywhere and did not need to exert himself. After the appearance of my biting polemic against Alexander Eliasberg—a man very well known at the time as a translator from the Russian, who had perpetrated a translation from the Yiddish with which just about everything was wrong—Strauss complimented me greatly and invited me to visit him, since he was himself working on a difficult translation. I went to see him and was very pleased to find in him a like-minded person in many things that occupied Zionists at that time. He inclined toward the same radical views on the Jews of Germany and their future, but he expressed them with a coolness and gentility that I could not achieve—qualities that spared him the vehement clashes that marked my path. Three months before the outbreak of the war he had gone to Palestine with his young wife with the intention of remaining there, but the war had forced him to return, like most of the Zionists who had come from Germany. Over a period of several years he had acquired a fairly good knowledge of Hebrew, but he did not feel secure with rabbinical Hebrew in particular and liked to consult people who were his superiors in this area and in that of Jewish lore. His feeling for the German language was extraordinary, and he planned to translate Agnon's first book, *Und das Krumme wird gerade* [And the Crooked Shall Be Made Straight], which had first appeared at Jaffa in 1912, in such a way as to preserve as far as possible the intonation and the structure of Agnon's Hebrew. Excerpts from it that had already appeared had attracted my attention. Rather frequent visits followed, and after I had been thrown out of my father's house I drew even closer to him. He told me about Agnon and finally brought us together at his home. He was the same age as Agnon, but he treated him with the greatest deference and respect, like a rare specimen of the species *homo sapiens*. This was entirely appropriate in the case of Agnon, an infinitely sensitive and complex human being.

Agnon came from Buczacz in Eastern Galicia, a Jewish *shtetl* that he helped immortalize in Hebrew literature. For four or five years he had lived in Eretz Yisrael, where he had definitively switched from Yiddish to Hebrew as his literary medium, and he had come to Germany in 1913. He intended to stay there for two or three years and explore literary possibilities in this new milieu. The outbreak of the war prolonged this temporary stay, and he did not return to Jerusalem until 1924. The German Jews were for him an inexhaustible object of critical astonishment, although he captivated a good many hearts among them. In his demeanor, and probably in his character as well, he was the virtual counterpole of Zalman Rubashov, whose expansive manner he lacked completely. Totally ignoring the abstract, he lived on an imaginative plane and expressed himself entirely through storytelling and in images, in his writings as well as in conversation. Every conversation with him quickly turned into one or more narratives, stories about great rabbis and simple Jews whose intonation he captured enchantingly. The same magic could be found even in his colorful but completely incorrect German. We liked each other. I found in him a new and altogether original incarnation of the Jewish spirit and of Jewish tradition (though he was by no means Orthodox in those days), and what attracted him to me was my passionate devotion to the sources and the seriousness with which I had studied Hebrew.

He attached great importance to drawing a distinction between Agnon the artist and Agnon the person. When I addressed him by his Hebrew *nom de plume* Agnon, he protested: "My name is Czaczkes." Agnon, he said, was a fine literary name, but how much could there be to a name which he had himself invented and which did not occur in the Holy Books? The name Czaczkes, on the other hand—and he undertook to prove this to me— was to be found among the mystical names of angels in the Book of Raziel, an ancient Hebrew book about angelology. His argumentation was not quite serious, but he stuck to it until he settled in Jerusalem. At that time I was a librarian at the Jewish National Library, and I told him that he would be registered under the name Agnon there and that it would be pointless to remonstrate.

Agnon was surrounded by an aura of solitude, a gentle melancholia, and more than a little Weltschmerz. He wrote many poems expressive of the spirit of loneliness. After the end of World War I, when we were both living in Munich, he read a number of them to me. They have all been burned, but among my papers there is one both in the original and in the German verse translation I made at that time.

I remember an evening in May 1917 at the Bet Ha'Va'ad

Ha'Ivri Klub [Hebrew Club] which was frequented almost exclusively by Russian, Polish, and Palestinian Jews.
Three or four German Jews also went there, and I was
probably the only native Berliner. On that evening Agnon
read one of his almost perfect stories, the *Aggadot Ha'Sofer*
[The Tale of the Scribe], which had not been printed yet
but was already being translated (and especially beautifully) into German by Max Strauss. I still remember the
profound impression which this story made. I can still
hear the echo of Agnon's delicate, plaintive voice reading
his story in a sort of interiorized monotonous singsong—
I almost said reeling off his story, for he was not a good
interpreter of his own works. And yet the rise and the fall
of his intonation was like an illustration of the words of
the poetess about "the languages notched like harps."

The Russian Jews with whom I lived in Pension Struck
were by nature and by character intellectuals, basically
enlighteners and enlightened people. Agnon, however,
had come from quite a distance, as it were, from a world
of images in which the springs of imagination flowed pro-
fusely. His conversations often enough were altogether
secular in nature, but he spoke in the style of his stories'
heroes, and there was something irresistibly magnetic
about this rhetorical style of speaking.

At that time Walter Benjamin was no longer in Berlin;
he had left the city early in April after his marriage,
and did not return for more than three years. Thus I
did not have the opportunity—as much as it would have
meant to me—to introduce him to Rubashov and Agnon,
those two *Ostjuden* whom I esteemed so highly. They
represented, almost symbolically, two opposite types of
the East European Jew.

VI

Jena (1917–1918)

My MILITARY PERIOD was short and stormy, and I do not wish to discuss it here. I rebelled against everything that went on there, and after a little more than two months I was discharged as a "psychopath" under the category "temporarily unfit for duty." The doctors summoned my father to Allenstein, where I was in training, and told him that the domestic conflict was partly to blame for my state. My father and I met and there was a reconciliation which, to be sure, was based on the condition that I would no longer live at home. I decided to continue my studies at the University of Jena, where several of my Heidelberg acquaintances had transferred in the meantime and so that I would not feel entirely alone.

The winter semester of 1917/18 was a very intensive one. Benjamin and his wife Dora—they had meanwhile gone to Switzerland—invited me to join them there. The very intense correspondence we engaged in over the next months excessively heightened the expectations we had of each other. The university itself had little that particu-

larly attracted me, but in nearby Halle my brother Werner
was in jail, having gotten off at the court-martial with nine
months' imprisonment for lese majesty, and I was able to
visit him there from time to time. Suspension proceedings
had been started against him at the University of Halle,
where he had been registered during his period of con-
valescence. At the behest of my brother I paid two calls
on the rector, the well-known liberal philosopher Hans
Vaihinger, author of *Die Philosophie des Als Ob* [The
Philosophy of As If], in order to plead his cause, and as I
recall, not without some success. When Vaihinger learned
that I was also studying philosophy and was reading Kant's
Critique of Judgment in Bruno Bauch's tutorial, he had a
friendly conversation with me about Kant. As the author
of the most comprehensive commentary on the *Critique
of Pure Reason,* he was a great authority in this field. He
did not say a word about the bitter conflict in which he
was then engaged with Bauch, a conflict that led to the
withdrawal of a nationalistic group from the Kant Society,
of which Vaihinger was the founding president.

Higher mathematics was weak at Jena, and I preferred
to study a few outstanding textbooks. The theologian
Willy Staerk read selections from the Psalms to a very
small number of students and did quite a good job. He
had a sonorous voice, and in his mouth Hebrew sounded
better than I have heard it pronounced by other theologians. My interest in the (philosophical?) foundations of
mathematics was amply stimulated by Gottlob Frege's
lectures—he was just about to retire—and the reading of
two of his publications. Frege surely was by far the most
important thinker of the School of Humanities, a man
who is world-famous to this day. At Jena he was merely an
appendage, barely tolerated and hardly taken seriously
by anyone. He was already in his late sixties, but I believe
he was not even a full professor yet. Paul F. Linke, a pupil

of Husserl and the second teacher who interested me
more than Bauch, was still a *Privatdozent* [adjunct lec-
turer] at the age of forty. Linke and Bauch were really at
opposite poles, professionally as well as personally. Bauch
was a courteous neo-Kantian, slightly condescending to
students, who was in the process of shifting camps from
Cohen to Rickert, while Linke was an exuberantly cheerful phenomenologist who was very open and obliging to
young people, though he was not particularly respected
as a member of his school. He was the only lecturer with
whom I established excellent personal relations in the
course of the winter. On the evenings we spent together
he gave marvelous recitations from the works of Christian
Morgenstern, the outstanding German writer of nonsense
poetry. Linke suggested that I write my dissertation
under his guidance on the foundations of mathematics,
even if I did not quite agree with his phenomenological
orientation. He could not very well ignore my reservations, for despite all my sympathy I strongly doubted the
refutation of the theory of relativity on the basis of *"reine
Wesensschau"* [intuition of essence], a refutation which
was prevalent among the phenomenologists then and even
years later. They held that Einstein's ideas were only
fictions in Vaihinger's sense—that is, "demonstrably" false
even though "fruitful." For this I had no use whatever,
and such intuition of essence was suspect to me.

As I have said earlier, I was not a member of the
Blau-Weiss organization, but in the summer of that year I
had published in its *Führerzeitung* [leaders' bulletin] a
sharp attack on the notions that prevailed there about
work with Jewish youth. The demands that I made and
my rather radical formulations of them were similar to
the ones made in that dispute at the Jüdisches Volksheim.
This led to closer contact with a few younger people from

the Leipzig Blau-Weiss who had been influenced by a speech, which they had invited me to give, to leave the association. We visited one another a number of times. Leipzig was the center of the German fur trade, which was almost entirely in Jewish and even predominantly Orthodox hands. With two exceptions my "fans" (who deserted me soon after I left Jena) were the children of influential (and affluent) Russian Jews in the fur trade. Thus I received a taste of the inner tensions as well as the human milieu of these families, for the parents found themselves confronted by the choice of either seeing their children go off to become Germans by assimilation or seeing them become Zionists. In Leipzig I also had a reunion with Agnon, who lived there for some time and visited me in Jena once or twice.

In Jena my only company at first were the female students I knew from Heidelberg and a few others whom they brought along. Some of us were in the same philosophy and mathematics classes and seminars, but above all we gathered every Friday evening in the large room in which I lived on Jenergasse, opposite the Botanical Garden. I often stood at the window staring at the beautiful garden landscape, which later in the term was usually covered with snow. There were two or three young men and six or seven young women, and we would read the Torah section for that Sabbath. (The Torah has always been divided in fifty-three sections—fifty-four in leap years—so it is read in its entirety in the synagogue in the course of one year.) I gave Hebrew lessons to my three Heidelberg ladies, and sometimes, depending on their progress, after the Sabbath candles had been lit we would read a few verses not only in German, but also in Hebrew.

To Käthe Holländer I owed two friendships. She often came with Käthe Ollendorf, who was a niece of the well-known theater critic Alfred Kerr and two years later

became the first wife of the expressionist poet Johannes
R. Becher. My Heidelberg friends were considerably
older than I, and none of them were exactly beauties.
Käthe Ollendorf, however, who was "already" twenty-
seven years old and was completing her medical studies,
was thoroughly charming and had an innocent expression
in her eyes that was absolutely unique. One could have
called her a "knockout," for that was the effect her glance
had on many. Yet she was a deeply religious person to
whom at bottom any faith appeared acceptable, though
the Jewish bacillus, which I probably was not the first to
implant in her, continued to be extremely active. She was
highly educated but totally unintellectual and completely
governed by her feelings. Above all, she was the most
disarming person I have ever met. For many years we
were friends, and in February 1933, when she happened
to visit us while on a Mediterranean trip, my wife and I
prevented her from returning to Germany. She did not
have the faintest comprehension of what was going on
there. In any case, she remained in Jerusalem as a physician
for almost forty years.

Outside the Friday evening meetings, Käthe Holländer
introduced me to an old friend of hers, Leni Czapski, a
young painter and the daughter of one of Ernst Abbe's
chief associates in the development of the Zeiss Works,
which next to the university was the great focal point of
Jena. This charming and vivacious creature was the child
of a mixed marriage and had been raised as a Christian. It
was I who introduced her to Judaism, and we remained
friends for years. Around 1925 she went to Kovno with
her husband, the expressionist painter Max Holzman.
Holzman, a Jew, was murdered there during the war, but
she survived with her daughter and visited me in Jerusalem
shortly before her death. One wonderful starry night
in late March of 1918 she and I walked back to Jena

after a visit to Weimar. She was the first person to paint my portrait.

But there was another acquaintance who was more impressive than anyone else in Jena. Due to the exigencies of wartime, there were more women than men in Bruno Bauch's major course on epistemology, which was supposed to build a bridge between Cohen, Windelband, and Rickert. One woman who was no longer quite so young attracted my attention because of her uncommonly fine bearing and what I would describe as the face of a noble damsel from feudal times. Yet her introspective expression made any approach impossible. It was a terrible winter; we went hungry and we froze. Students were alloted a small ration of coal, which we had to pick up at the distribution center and cart away ourselves. One day when I happened to be coming down the street I saw her pushing her cart laboriously up the hill. I went up to her, introduced myself as a fellow student in Bauch's course, and asked her to let me help her. She gave me a somewhat searching look and then answered in the affirmative. Thus I took her coal to a district located on a hill on the other side of the Saale, and she invited me to have tea with her. She said: "I am Katharina Gentz, and this is my roommate, Alice Heymann." Miss Heymann, who had delicate, markedly Jewish features and looked just as sickly as she actually was, lay on the chaise longue most of the time. I glanced around a bit and asked whether I might look at a pile of papers that lay at the head of the couch. To my extreme surprise I found there a copy of Walter Benjamin's manuscript *Über zwei Gedichte von Hölderlin* [On Two Poems by Hölderlin], which he had distributed to only a few people and which I had received from him two years previously in the same kind of envelope. "Oh, yes," said Alice, "he and I were together in the Freie Studentenschaft in Freiburg and Berlin, and he gave it to me in the spring of 1915." Since then she had had no contact with him. We both had reason to take an interest in each other.

But I found Katharina Gentz, the first non-Jewish girl with whom I struck up a friendship, far more impressive. She actually did have the kind of austere personality that one connects with those ladies in medieval chambers whom one sees in German paintings from the fifteenth century. She was not tall but very slender, and she spoke few words—and those slowly—but what she said was precise and always to the point. We exchanged family histories. When she was born in 1890 in Wriezen (on the Oder marshes), her father, the principal of a *Realschule,* was already sixty-five years old. Like many female students of that generation, she had taken the teaching examinations and worked in elementary schools before she had decided to study at a university. She studied German language and literature and later became a *Studienrätin* [secondary-school teacher] in Frankfurt am Main, where I visited her ten years later, and in Kiel. On long evenings we often spoke about Germans and Jews, the war, literature, and moral philosophy. She knew a great deal about art, but I was not sufficiently conversant with that field to hold my own in such a conversation. But almost always when I came to see her and her friend, the reproductions hanging in her room had been changed. I have met quite a few people in my life who were well composed, but this girl possessed that quality to a superlative degree. Not that she knew the answers to the mysteries of the universe, far from it; but she exuded an indescribable tranquility and her great reserve masked an immense human openness. Her older brother was a district attorney and had had many bad experiences in his work, some of them involving Jews. The semester after I left Jena two of my friends from Jung Juda came to study there, and Katharina Gentz "inherited" them from me. Her brother's attitude toward Jews changed markedly through his acquaintance with this Jewish circle, to which his sister introduced him. Katharina became engaged to one of these two friends. When he came to Eretz Yisrael one year after I did, I saw the engagement ring on his right hand and asked, "Who is it?" "Katharina," he replied. She was nine years his senior, but she was prepared to come and live with him in Eretz Yisrael. Their relationship changed later on, but their friendship lasted all their lives and is still intact after sixty years.

That eventful fall and winter also saw the beginning of my friendship with Werner Kraft, with whom I started corresponding during my military period at the suggestion of Walter Benjamin. Kraft suffered tremendously because of the circumstances of the times and his assignment in Hannover as a medical orderly fit only for garrison duty. Benjamin wrote me that he and his wife were greatly worried about Kraft, who was twenty-one at the time. He actually did come close to committing suicide, as evidenced by his disconsolate and profoundly melancholy letters, and his poems were also suffused with despair. I remember writing to him imploringly to keep him from that final act. Once he spent two or three days with me in Jena where he met Toni Halle, his future sister-in-law. We had exciting conversations and became friends.

Kraft had an entirely different orientation from mine. Jewish matters were very far from his mind in those days, and he once wrote me how deeply touched he had been to meet a person like me who really cared about Judaism. He had forgotten that he had written a letter to Walter

Benjamin in the fall of 1916 in which he made unfriendly remarks about Judaism, whereupon Benjamin, who had been reading Achad Ha'am at my suggestion, wrote him in no uncertain terms that he was loyal to Judasim and even considered going to Palestine after the war. In late December 1916 Kraft answered that this avowal of Judaism had greatly surprised him and that the sole explanation he could think of was the influence of a woman. I can still picture the meaningful wink with which Benjamin read that letter to me. Even then Kraft's stars in the literary firmament—and he really lived exclusively in that world—were Karl Kraus and Rudolf Borchardt. He corresponded with Benjamin about these men and wrote long unpublished treatises on them, some of which I had a chance to read. These two writers were both Jews, but motivated by entirely different impulses they had completely turned away from Judaism. Borchardt was a nationalistic advocate of traditional conservatism; during the war he even turned annexationist. Kraus was the most fanatical, most eloquent, and the most vocal spokesman against the war. He was the sole writer for *Die Fackel* [The Torch], a journal about which the most astonishing, indeed almost miraculous thing was that it could be published at all. (I became acquainted with this journal in the spring of 1916 through a Zionist acquaintance who not only recommended its contents to me but also advised me to learn German prose from it; from that time on I read it almost regularly.) When I left for Switzerland, our correspondence, which was sometimes very hectic, assumed more moderate form. When Kraft married Toni Halle's sister in 1922, I was (as I had been at Benjamin's wedding) perhaps the only person who was not related to the families concerned but had been invited by both as a friend. The ceremony was conducted by Rabbi Leo Baeck, who was regarded as the outstanding figure among the Berlin rabbinate. This was our first encounter, and it was followed by many more until his death.

On the fifth of December I turned twenty. That afternoon I sat alone in my room and thought about myself. The doorbell rang, and the mailman appeared with a special-delivery letter from Walter Benjamin, the likes of which I never received from him again. It was a brief reply to a remark that I had made about the manuscript of his essay on Dostoyevsky's *The Idiot;* at the same time it contained his good wishes for my birthday. I had interpreted that essay as an esoteric comment on his dead friend Fritz Heinle. I cannot describe my youth without quoting these few lines, which played a great role in our relationship. The letter begins without a salutation.

Since receiving your letter I have often found myself in a festive mood. It is as though I have entered a holiday season, and I must celebrate with reverence the revelation in that which has made itself known to you. For it simply is the case that what has reached you and you alone must have been addressed to you and has entered our life again for a moment. I have entered a new phase of my life, for that which severed me from all people with planetary speed and turned even my closest relationships except for my marriage into shadows unexpectedly emerges and establishes a connection at a different place.

That is all I will write you today, although this letter is supposed to be your birthday letter as well.

Yours, Walter Benjamin

At the beginning of January 1918 I was summoned to a re-examination in Weimar, where I was classified as "permanently unfit for active duty; not to be examined further," which meant that my name was removed from the personnel roster. Since the army was no longer interested in me, I now had a real chance to get to Switzerland. I asked my mother to visit me in Jena and presented my situation to her. Could she induce my father to give me permission to go to Berne—where the Benjamins were waiting for me—for the "restoration" of my health and continuation of my studies? My mother understood the situation very well and said: "Leave it to me; I'll speak with Father, but it will take a little time." By the end of February she had obtained his consent. Dr. Karl Meyer, a friend of ours in Switzerland whom my mother and I had met on two vacations in 1913 and 1914 when he was working as a spa doctor, declared in writing that he was ready to take care of me if I came to Switzerland. Armed with this document and my military papers, I went to see the district medical officer in Jena and received a certificate saying that there were no objections to my leaving for Switzerland. Without such certification it was impossible to receive a passport in those days. All this paper work took weeks to complete. The semester came to an end; I took leave of my friends, who envied me my good fortune, and then went to Berlin for a few days where I was able to leave my library with my uncle. It had already grown to considerable dimensions.

VII

Berne (1918–1919)

ON MAY 4, 1918, I crossed the border at Friedenshafen. I cannot describe the sense of euphoria that suffused me as I stood on the Lake Constance steamer bound for Romanshorn and looked back at Germany. The war was over for me. At eight o'clock that evening, Walter Benjamin met me at the station in Berne.

I stayed in Berne for about a year and a half, and thus experienced the great events—the end of the war and the so-called German revolution as well as everything that followed—only from the outside and without deeper involvement. Of course, the armistice was a turning point of far-reaching importance for me as well. In my book on Walter Benjamin I have given a detailed account of this Swiss period to the extent that it concerns my central relationship with him. Here I will speak of some aspects that did not belong in that context.

At the university, which was exceedingly quiet, petit-bourgeois, and not very distinguished, I studied almost exclusively mathematics, theoretical physics, and philoso-

phy. In addition I began to study Arabic under Karl
Marti, an Old Testament scholar very well known at that
time, and I took his seminar on the Book of Job, in
which every participant had to read a verse aloud each
session. When my turn would come, Marti would say:
"Herr Scholem, don't read so fast." Marti was a man with
an uncommon liking for the Jews and their history; he
was very friendly to the Jewish students, almost all of
whom were from Russia or Galicia. Mathematicians of
the caliber of the Berlin scholars were not to be found
here. But one of them gave a magnificent course on some
difficult aspects of the theory of numbers. He was a
Privatdozent by the name of Berliner, a Russian Jew
whom I saw in the synagogue on Friday evenings for
some months where he said Kaddish, the prayer for the
dead in the year of mourning, for one of his parents.

Both my conversations with Benjamin and my own
special interests often led to cursory or intensive readings. The Swiss Landesbibliothek [national library] had
many unexpected philosophical treasures, but there were
also scholarly works about the Bible and many dissertations on Judaic subjects that had been produced at Swiss
universities by Jewish students from Eastern Europe,
some of them no longer young. My greatest surprise,
to be sure, lay between the two areas of interest. One
of the greatest names in contemporary Hebrew letters
was Micha Josef Berdyczevski, the intellectual antipode
of Achad Ha'am and champion of Jewish modernism. In
Berdyczevski, one of the most influential Hebrew writers
to this day, the conflict between tradition and a complete
new beginning had crystallized in its most pronounced
form. I was already familiar with his Hebrew writings,
in which he had been the first to make known the work
of Nietzsche. Two volumes of his great and excellent

work *Die Sagen der Juden* [The Legends of the Jews] had already appeared. Like all his scholarly works published in German, it appeared under the name Micha Josef bin Gorion, and it is undoubtedly one of the most valuable Judaic source books in the German language. (It is, incidentally, the principal and most exploited source for Thomas Mann's novel *Joseph and His Brothers.*) I was greatly interested in this author, who, strangely enough, seemed to have established two distinct fields of work, one in Hebrew and one in German. I had seen him only once in Louis Lamm's secondhand Hebrew bookshop in Berlin; Lamm had whispered to me, "That is Dr. Berdyczevski." Only in Berne, as I was browsing through a collection of Berne dissertations as a member of the philosophical seminar, did I find his dissertation, which I had often searched for and which had always eluded me. It was a fifty-page outline of a philosophical system!

As regards my further Jewish education, however, I owe most to a medical student who was a *rara avis* among the Jewish students from Eastern Europe in Berne, for he was still strictly Orthodox. David Schklar was a brilliant Talmudist who also spoke excellent Hebrew. He suggested that I study Talmud with him twice a week, and I did so for almost a year and with great pleasure. He had a keen mind, but he was difficult and a bit crazy. Forty years later he came to Israel from Canada as an elderly physician.

While the number of Jewish students in Switzerland had been considerable before the Russian Revolution, the majority returned to Russia in 1917 (via France, Holland, and Sweden). Another large group, those who had publicly or perceptibly demonstrated their sympathies for the new rulers, were expelled from Switzerland when they did not leave the country of their own accord. Thus I found only a diminished number of Russo-Jewish students, and I met with some of them on a number of occasions. Some still betrayed traces of cured tuberculosis; the one I liked best among them died of that disease shortly after I left. Otherwise I had little personal intercourse other than my intense association with Walter and Dora Benjamin. The few people with whom I did associate included the very pious Waldhaus family from Eastern Europe, whom I liked best to visit at the end of the Sabbath because they sang Hebrew and Aramaic hymns with very beautiful Hasidic melodies. There was also the niece of my medical protector Karl Meyer; during my stay she married one of the very few "native" Swiss Zionists, Herr Bollag. He was a Jew who, like herself, came from one of the two Swiss Jewish villages, Endingen and Lengnau, the only villages in which Jews were allowed to live on Swiss soil over a period of more than two centuries. It was a long time before I met other "autochthonous" Swiss Zionist families and made friends among them.

Here it is high time to introduce my cousin Leonie Ortenstein, called Lony, whom I found at a place which one would hardly expect in this context, namely the German Legation at Berne. She was one of the daughters of the mixed marriage in the Pflaum family which I mentioned near the beginning of my narrative. We had, of course, known each other since childhood, but at the age of nineteen she had contracted a severe case of tuberculosis and in 1916 had been sent to Davos as a terminal case. But to everyone's surprise, including her own, she recovered, was able to leave the "magic mountain," and found a position as secretary to the head of a newly established office for the procurement of fats at the German Legation in Berne. As long as I lived next door to Benjamin, in a large attic room in the postman's house

overlooking a marvelous cornfield in the village of Muri
(which at that time still lay outside the city limits), Lony
and I saw little of each other. But when I moved to the city
in the fall and took a room not very far from her place, we
got together often and became very good friends.

Lony, who was only a year older than I, was nearly my
exact opposite in every way. She was an almost pure
aesthete who ate as frugally as possible but spent a lot of
money for a beautiful and elegant apartment and clothes
to match. She had hardly any convictions; the experiences
of a difficult youth—she had been an early orphan and a
poor relation at the homes of rich uncles—had left no
room for convictions, and her skeptical and purely con-
templative nature seemed to preclude them as well. She
took cognizance of my very definite convictions with
interest but also with equanimity. She was cheerful but not
witty, friendly but hardly familiar, and she liked being
courted; she never lacked for admirers, either, although
(with one exception) she never responded to them seriously in any way. She was not what one would have called
beautiful, but she had much charm, and, as far as I was able
to determine, she loved only flowers, music, and books.
The story was told that at the Bollag–Meyer wedding I
had appeared with a big bouquet of roses, held it in my
hand the whole time, and then left still holding it; this is
said to have attracted attention and aroused merriment.
Probably I had brought the flowers for Lony.

In those days everyone, and certainly every woman, was
reading Agnes Günther's big and literarily pretentious
bestseller *Die Heilige und ihr Narr* [The Saint and Her
Fool], and Lony would not leave me in peace until I had
read that fat novel. Today, if I am not mistaken, it is
regarded as classic kitsch, although I am not absolutely
certain that this judgment is correct. In the case of enor-
mously successful works of this kind, one is not quite

sure which side of high literature they belong to, and critical opinion is often all too obviously dependent on the prevailing atmosphere and orientation. It was similar with André Schwarz-Bart's prize-winning (Prix Goncourt) novel *The Last of the Just,* which was published almost twenty years after the Holocaust. The emotional appeal it made was akin to that of the earlier book, and it moved all its readers to tears. Being mad about Judaica, I gave Lony the German edition of Agnon's *Und das Krumme wird gerade* to read in order to give her an idea of what I regarded as truly great literature (and a great translation). She liked the book, and to show her appreciation she had Professor Marti's daughter make a wonderful vellum binding for my copy, which is still in my library.

She was for me an ideal counterpart to Walter Benjamin. With Benjamin there were profound discussions and exchanges of ideas, struggles for convictions, and sparks that were kindled in both of us. Lony, on the other hand, was a pure receptacle, or rather, a listener *par excellence.* She attentively listened to my effusions without my having to expect rejoinders. Walter and Dora, whom I took her to see a few times, were charmed by her as well. In a word, she somehow lived outside the world, but live she did. Her presence was palpable. She also brought me together with the two typically Swiss musicians who were courting her. Soon after I left Switzerland she did become engaged to the younger of these, a highly gifted conductor from a Basel family that was *piekfein* [ritzy], to use a Berlinism. The family raised vehement objections to the engagement: "Surely you are not going to bring a Jewess into our house!" The mother refused to even receive the girl, and the engagement was broken off.

In February and March of 1919, Elsa Burchhardt came to Berne and I had a new person to talk to. (I had met her toward the end of January 1918 on a visit to Heidelberg.)

She became friends with the Benjamins as well as with Lony. Lony, who later lived in the Eternal City until her death ten days before the Allies' capture of Rome, remained in close touch with us until the outbreak of World War II and once came to visit us in Jerusalem. She was the secretary of the German delegate to the International Agricultural Institute who somehow—I don't know how—kept her on even during the Nazi period despite all objections. Was she a German? Was she a Jew? I believe she herself did not know.

My interest in the Kabbala—Jewish mysticism—manifested early on, and probably very varied motives were responsible for it. Perhaps I was endowed with an affinity for this area from the "root of my soul," as the kabbalists would have put it, or maybe my desire to understand the enigma of Jewish history was also involved—and the existence of the Jews over the millennia *is* an enigma, no matter what the numerous "explanations" may say. Like almost all the founders of the Science of Judaism in the last century (Zunz, Rapoport, Luzzatto, Geiger, and Steinschneider), Graetz, whose *History of the Jews* had so entranced me, displayed the greatest aversion to everything connected with religious mysticism. He calls the classic work of the Spanish Kabbala, the Zohar, a book of lies, and whenever he speaks of the kabbalists he employs a whole dictionary of invectives. I could not say why, but it seemed improbable to me that the kabbalists could have been such charlatans, buffoons, and masters of tomfoolery as he made them out to be. Something seemed to me to be hidden there, and it was this that attracted me. The lasting impression which Buber's first two volumes on Hasidism made on me surely played a part as well. Still wholly written in the style of the Vienna School and of the *Jugendstil* [the German version of *art nouveau,* ca. 1895–1905], they drew attention to this area in romantic transfiguration and flowery metaphors.

From 1915 on I timorously began to read books about the Kabbala, and later I tried my hand at original texts of kabbalistic and Hasidic literature. This was fraught with great difficulties in Germany at that time, for though it was always possible to find Talmud scholars, there was nobody to guide one in this field. Once I tried to induce Dr. Bleichrode to read such a text with a few of us; it was a famous treatise on kabbalistic ethics from the sixteenth century. After a few hours he said: *"Kinderlach,* we have to give it up. I don't understand the quotations from the Zohar [the book was full of them] and can't explain things to you properly." Thus I had to try to become familiar with these sources by myself. After all, though the Zohar was written in Aramaic, it was no more intricate than, say, the writings of Johann Georg Hamann, several volumes of which I had in my room. I bought myself an edition of the Zohar and tried my luck. I read the four volumes of Molitor's work *Philosophie der Geschichte oder Über die Tradition* [Philosophy of History, or On Tradition] (1827–53) which was actually about the Kabbala and was then still obtainable from the publisher for a song. It became clear to me that the Christological reinterpretations of this author, a pupil of Schelling and Baader, were completely wrongheaded, but that he did know more about the subject than the Judaic authorities of his time. I also read S.A. Horodezky's Hebrew writings on Hasidism, which at that time were almost the only works in modern Hebrew literature on the great holy men of Hasidism. In Berne I learned that Horodezky was living there, and I paid him a call. He was twenty-five years older than I. He received me in a very friendly fashion, and immediately suggested that I translate several chapters from his Hebrew manuscript (he could not write

German) for a projected major German study on this subject. While I was working on the translation, I realized that there was something wrong with these writings and that their author was a rather unperceptive panegyrist.

Between 1915 and 1918 I filled quite a few notebooks with excerpts, translations, and reflections on the Kabbala, though these were still far from being scholarly efforts and insights. But the bacillus had taken hold, and in the spring of 1919 the various developments which I have tried to outline here led to my decision to shift the focus of my studies from mathematics to Judaic studies externally as well and to begin a scholarly study of the Kabbala, at least for a few years. I had no idea at that time that these projected few years would become a lifetime occupation; I had other Judaic aspirations in mind, such as a book about the literature, the function, and the metaphysics of the elegy (Kinah) in Hebrew literature. I had already made a series of studies on that subject, and in Der Jude I had published a translation, which is dear to me even today, of a moving medieval elegy about the burning of the Talmud in Paris in 1240.

My decision at the same time determined the choice of a university once I returned to Germany. Earlier I had considered completing my mathematical studies at Göttingen, the mathematicians' mecca. Now the only choice was Munich where there was, and still is, Germany's largest collection of Hebrew manuscripts, including many kabbalistic writings. The fact that Elsa Burchhardt had in the meantime also gone to Munich made my decision even easier.

To be sure, the universities did not encourage Jewish studies in those days. Today, when there are hardly any Jews left in Germany, many German universities want to establish a chair of Judaic studies. But at that time, when

Germany had a lively Jewish population that was in great ferment, no university and no state ministry would hear of it. There was no dearth of such attempts over a period of a hundred years, but all of them failed. What Heinrich Heine wrote is quite true: If there were only one Jew in the world, everyone would come running to see him, but now that there are too many, people try to avert their eyes. I, however, wanted to make an attempt to unlock these mysterious texts, written in peculiar symbols, and make them comprehensible—to myself or to others. In summer 1919 I conceived of a subject that was suggested by my reading of this literature up to that time and appeared materially fruitful and philosophically relevant to me: the linguistic theory of the Kabbala. That was youthful exuberance, if not arrogance. When I tackled the project in earnest, I had soon to realize that I did not know nearly enough and had better start more systematically and, above all, more modestly. In point of fact, I wrote the study on the linguistic theory of the Kabbala, which I resignedly abandoned in 1920, exactly fifty years later.

VIII

Munich (1919–1922)

IN SEPTEMBER 1919, I returned to Germany. Thanks to extreme thriftiness I had been able to save a few hundred
francs from my stipend. To be sure, I overdid things
somewhat—for weeks on end I ate only fried eggs with
fried potatoes in a cheap restaurant—and the price I paid
for such excesses was a vitamin deficiency. My medical
guardian angel, Dr. Meyer, took me aside at his niece's
wedding and said: "Gerhard, what is the matter with you? I
don't like your looks. Come to see me tomorrow morning,
before I go back to Leysin." As a consequence he wrote a
letter to Berlin saying that I had to eat better, and thus I
received fifty additional francs each month. In the fall I
took my savings to the two secondhand book dealers in
Berlin that specialized in Judaica and bought kabbalistic
writings. Among them was a French translation of the
Zohar that had appeared in Paris between 1906 and 1912
in six thick volumes. It was the work of a mysterious
person who called himself Jean de Pauly, and it had been
printed by France's biggest paper manufacturer, Emile

Lafuma-Giraud, on wonderful paper made expressly for this one book (which bore the Hebrew name of God as a watermark!). The reason I tell this story is to indicate the state of Kabbala scholarship at that time. The situation became clear to me when I made the following statement in Munich: that this universally praised *chef d'oeuvre*, which was quoted everywhere and served as the basis for entire books, was a useless, blatant piece of botchwork by a half-educated swindler from Eastern Galicia. It was brimful of brazen fabrications and included, among other things, a 450-page volume of notes that consisted from beginning to end of fictitious quotations and scholarly references to nonexisting books or nonexisting chapters in well-known kabbalistic classics. No one had ever done any checking, and no one would believe me at the time. I was asked how I knew that these books did not even exist. Such were my beginnings.

In Munich I managed to find a large room at 98 Türkenstrasse, near the Siegestor [Victory Arch] and directly opposite the Akademie der Künste [Academy of the Arts]. My landlady kept only one room of her big apartment for herself and rented all the others. I also found a room for my cousin Heinz Pflaum, who had just begun his studies in Romance languages and literatures. The room opposite his was already occupied by the graphic artist Tom Freud, about whom I shall have more to say later. We made up a small Zionist colony: my cousin was to come to Jerusalem three years after my emigration and would become the first professor of Romance languages and literatures there. In my room I had considerable space for books; some of them came from my Berlin library, while others were gradually acquired from the very well stocked secondhand bookshops of Munich.

I took one last course in mathematics with the famous

Alfred Pringsheim, but I really concentrated on philosophy and Semitics, which last I was considering as a second minor subject. I planned to take my doctorate in philosophy with a dissertation on "The Linguistic Philosophy of the Kabbala." In Clemens Bäumker I found a distinguished historian of medieval philosophy, whose favor I won in his seminar on the *quaestio de anima* [dissertation on the soul] of Thomas Aquinas. He was interested in medieval Jewish thought and encouraged me in my studies. I came to see him at the end of the seminar in March 1920, and he agreed to accept my doctoral dissertation on this area of the Kabbala, which he himself called a scholarly *terra incognita*. As I have already mentioned, I had in the meantime become more modest and proposed to undertake an edition and translation with commentary of the oldest extant and exceedingly difficult kabbalistic text, the Sefer Ha-Bahir. Bäumker was very much in favor of this, but he told me that in Munich it was possible to get a degree with a major in philosophy only if psychology was taken as a minor—a subject to which I had taken a hearty dislike. "That doesn't matter, Mr. Scholem; I shall speak with my colleague Becher." But I could not stand colleague Becher, whose field of specialization was brain weights. My general dislike of the subject was only increased by my study of phenomenological analyses of psychological problems which were then very fashionable. In those days I came to reject the phenomenology of Husserl, though I had been greatly in sympathy with it for a few years, having been impressed by the very subtle *Logische Untersuchungen (Logical Investigations)*. But the lectures of Husserl's disciple Wilhelm Pfänder completely alienated me from this mode of thinking. In a public lecture—I myself was present—Pfänder performed the feat of making the existence of God (which I have never doubted) "visible" by phenomenological means. This was too much for me. His seminar also helped to drive me out of this circle. Once a dead serious discussion extended over several hours in the presence of some very penetrating minds (I still remember Maximilian Beck), concerning the question whether a fried fish was a fish or not. I should add, though, that Benjamin's intellectual perspective, with which I had such close contact in those years and which was the farthest thing imaginable from what one could call academic philosophy, prevented me from taking very seriously university teachers of philosophy who were not historians.

Thus, at Bäumker's advice I changed my major to Semitics. There I received a very friendly reception from Fritz Hommel (in whose readings of Arabic texts and seminar I was already enrolled), though Hommel had accepted a dissertation in Judaica only once in his long career. Bäumker and Hommel were already over sixty-five—the one a devout Catholic, the other an equally devout Protestant, a very pious Lutheran. Hommel was primarily an Assyriologist, but he was generous enough to exempt me from this particular area of Semitics and asked only that my major include Arabic and Ethiopian in addition to Hebrew and Aramaic, with which I was already conversant. In his life as a scholar he was at the center of numerous polemics. During the two and a half years that I was his student we were on the best of terms.

In the first winter semester in Munich the Catholic Old Testament scholar Göttsberger announced a discussion course entitled "Readings in the Babylonian Talmud." Together with Elsa Burchhardt and Rudolf Hallo, I went to see what the course would be like. All the other students were Catholic seminarians. I should point out here that the text of the Talmud has no punctuation, and one of the difficulties in the study of the Talmud is to determine whether one is dealing with a statement or a question. At the very beginning the professor made a bad blunder. I raised my hand and said: "Professor, that is not a statement but a question." "How do you know?" asked the professor. "It says so in Rashi," I replied, "and is a centuries-old tradition." "Rabbinical sophistry!" With this the professor closed the discussion. Thus we realized with amusement that nothing was to be learned from that gentleman. In Munich, however, there was an excellent Talmudist with whom we studied the tractate on marriage contracts for an hour a day—in summer in the early morning after the morning prayer in the synagogue, in winter in the afternoon in his apartment. This subject may sound strange, but the tractate is actually one of the most interesting and most varied. It was popularly known as "the little Talmud," because it contained, so to speak, everything. It is 112 leaves in length, and in those Munich years I "learned" it from beginning to end. Dr. Heinrich Ehrentreu who, like many rabbis in Germany, had come from Hungary, was the rabbi of the small Orthodox synagogue association that rejected the organ in the large synagogue situated not far from the Stachus square. He was a first-rate scholar, looked the way one imagines a Talmudic sage would look, and was an even-tempered and peaceable person. In this he was quite different from the younger generation of Orthodox Jews, who were very aggressive in nature. These Jews began to go to the severely anti-Zionist yeshivas of Hungary and Lithuania for their Talmudic studies, and often came back greatly changed after a year or two. Ehrentreu, who liked me, knew that I was not Orthodox. But one of his sons who came from Galanta during his vacation refused to shake hands with me and reproachfully asked his father how he could tolerate a heretic like me in his Talmud course. "The light in the Torah will lead him to what is good," said his father, quoting from the Talmud. Bleichrode and Ehrentreu were the two teachers of my youth whom I remember with the greatest gratitude.

I read Maimonides's philosophical work *Guide for the Perplexed* together with Escha (Elsa Burchhardt), who came from an Orthodox Hamburg doctor's family, and with Leo Wislicki, a student from Kattowitz [Katowice], who was four years younger and my fellow student in Ehrentreu's study group. (Wislicki later became a professor of pharmacology in Jerusalem and has been a friend in Ehrentreu's spirit to this day.) Since I was simultaneously studying Arabic syntax, I was fortunately able to cope more easily with the literal imitation of the Arabic syntax in the Hebrew translation, which often proves detrimental to an understanding of Maimonides's work. Most of my time, to be sure, I spent in the manuscript department of the Bavarian State Library, where my table was garnished with Hebrew codices and printed works. At the next table sat an uncommonly slender man, my senior by perhaps ten years, with the unmistakable sharply contoured and intense face of a Jewish intellectual. His table was piled high with German manuscripts, and he generally took his seat, as I did, shortly after the reading room opened. He was Eduard Berend from Hannover, the outstanding Jean Paul scholar, who was here preparing his critical edition of my one favorite among the German classical writers. Once I confessed my love for Jean Paul to him, and he said: "Sometime why don't you give me some information on all those rabbinical stories in Jean Paul." Jean Paul and Paul Scheerbart were the only German authors whose collected works I took along to Eretz Yisrael. In a handbook of contemporary literature published in 1905, which Werner Kraft showed me just a few days before these lines were written, I read this all-too-true sentence in the entry on

Scheerbart: "The least-read important author of contemporary literature because he is the only completely un-
erotic one." And this was written by none other than
Hanns Heinz Ewers!* Since no one read Scheerbart, I
was able to purchase many of his writings, among them
wonderful and hard-to-find ones, for a song in the secondhand bookshops of Munich.

In Munich I met two girls from my Jena circle, Toni
Halle and Käthe Ollendorf; the latter's marriage to
Johannes R. Becher was just breaking up. There was also
Gustav Steinschneider, with whom I had been in the
same army platoon in 1917 and whose fate particularly
touched Escha and me. He was the grandson of the
greatest Hebrew bibliographer and manuscript expert of
the last century, a man who at a ripe old age freely
admitted that he regarded it as the function of the
Wissenschaft vom Judentum [Science of Judaism] to provide a decent burial for this important but declining
phenomenon. Surely Moritz Steinschneider was the first
authority in this field who was admittedly an agnostic and
possibly even an atheist. I was a great admirer of this
stupendous scholar, and if I had played in the Friedrichs-
hain instead of the Märkischer Park as a boy, I could have
seen the nonagenarian sitting there on a bench. In
those days I reflected quite a bit about this group of
scholarly liquidators, and in 1921 I planned to write an
article about the suicide of Judaism being carried out by
the so-called Science of Judaism for Benjamin's periodical *Angelus Novus,* a journal that never appeared.
    Gustav came from a family constellation that was similar
to mine. His father was one of the leading members of the
Berlin Monistenbund [association of monists], which at

*Ewers (1871–1943) wrote novels and stories full of sex and satanism.
—Trans.

that time was probably the best-known organization of leftist atheists; the sons of its members were asked to join the "Sonne" [Sun], the association's youth group. Gustav's older brother became a communist and his younger brother an ardent Zionist and one of the first German *halutzim* [agricultural pioneers] who went to Eretz Yisrael. Gustav himself, a very quiet and thoughtful man, vacillated between the two camps. Like his younger brother Karl, he had a natural dignity and was very musical, but was utterly unworldly and incapable of doing anything "practical." His speech was tremendously slow and he spoke with a melodious drawl. We shared a room in the Allenstein army barracks. As everyone knows, even then the most active word in a soldier's vocabulary was *"Scheisse"* [shit]. Gustav was the first and last person whom I have heard pronounce this word in an inimitable way—as though it were a German linguistic treasure and could have formed part of the cultic language of Stefan George and his circle. He inclined to hypochondria, and his thin, somewhat weary face betrayed the potential philosopher. Gustav was reading books I had never heard of, and over the years he recommended to me the writings of an expressionistic philosopher named Adrien Turel who was a frequent visitor to the Steinschneider family. I did not understand a word of Turel's writings. In the four years before my emigration Gustav and I were on very friendly relations; it may have been the almost complete polarity of our characters that attracted us to each other. He spent the first year at Munich with us, and Escha and I strove—unsuccessfully, of course—to persuade him to take some definite course of studies. After 1933 it took the highest kind of "pull"—the intercession of my friend Zalman Rubashov with the mayor of Tel Aviv—to procure for Gustav (and other Ph.D.'s and artists in every imaginable field) a position as a streetsweeper.

His nocturnal employment permitted him to philosophize by day or (later) to play four-handed duets with my aunt, a pianist trained by Konrad Ansorge. As a streetsweeper, incidentally, Gustav was highly respected and popular among his colleagues. That was one of the occupations in which a knowledge of Hebrew was not important.

After Heinz Pflaum had left for Heidelberg, Escha moved into his room on Türkenstrasse. Opposite her room at the end of the corridor lived the graphic artist and book illustrator Tom Freud, a niece of Sigmund Freud and one of the unforgettable figures of those years. In contrast to her somewhat older sister Lilly Marlé, who was married to the actor Arnold Marlé and often came to visit her, Tom was ugly in an almost picturesque way. The two Marlés were members of the company at the Kammerspiele and often gave dramatic readings, especially at Jewish events. Lilly was an outstanding beauty and looked the way painters and etchers then liked to portray the protagonist of the biblical Book of Ruth. Tom was a brilliant illustrator of children's books; in some cases she also wrote the text. Agnon, who lived in Munich in the winter of 1919–1920 and often came to see us, had written a Hebrew children's book in which each letter of the alphabet was described and glorified in longish verses. The book was scheduled to be published by the German Zionist Association in a large edition, and Tom Freud had been engaged as its illustrator. Thus Agnon had three reasons to visit the same apartment when he came to confer with Tom about the illustrations. Tom lived only on cigarettes, so to speak, and her room was usually filled with smoke, though this bothered Agnon and other visitors less than it did me. The older I got, the less I could stand smoke-filled rooms, and it took a lively interest to induce me to stay in her room for any length of time. She was an authentic bohemian, and had a good many contacts with artists and writers. It was in her room that I carried on a vehement conversation about Zionism with Otto Flake, then a very well-known writer who lived not far from us. Flake, a very slender, very good-looking and elegant man, was at that time a member of the German liberal left and an advocate of the total assimilation of German Jewry, something that he expected to produce great benefits for the Germans. I was certainly the wrong person to whom to express such views, and our conversation reflected that. Unless I am mistaken, he later no longer regarded the matter as so simple.

At that time Agnon was about to marry Esther Marx, the beautiful daughter of what might be described as one of the most aristocratic Orthodox Jewish families of Germany, a family whose fame has endured to this day. Esther Marx had two qualities I deemed especially memorable in those days: she was as much a confirmed atheist as she was an admirer and master of the Hebrew language—surely a rare combination among German Jews. She spent that winter at Starnberg, and Agnon proudly showed me her postcards, which were written in flawless calligraphy and almost flawless Hebrew. During that time I translated into German a good number of Agnon's shorter stories, some of them from manuscript, including a few of his most perfect writings which later appeared in *Der Jude*. We frequently took walks in Munich, especially along the Isar and in the English Garden, and Agnon, a tireless conversationalist, expounded on his particular likes and dislikes in Hebrew literature, above all on the contemporary scene. I probably talked a lot also. We often conversed about German Jewry as well, displaying critical detachment from it in quite different forms. In those days Agnon had become friends with several German intellectuals, and he used to treat me to panegyrics about them. To tell the truth, Agnon, who came from another country, intuitively had a better and deeper understanding for many Germans than I did. Most of the time we spoke Hebrew, which I did not often have the opportunity to do in my Munich years. Only occasionally did Ariel Avigdor come to the city, and then we would talk at length in Hebrew about our future life in Eretz Yisrael. He was the son of one of the founders of the Jewish village of Gedera, who had become a hydraulic engineer and was preparing for his activities in Eretz Yisrael at a big power station near Munich.

On my way back from Switzerland I visited Martin Buber at Heppenheim. This time, however, I was sensible enough not to go by way of Lake Constance, but to take the "boring" route via Basel and Frankfurt. Buber highly approved of my decision to turn to the investigation of the Kabbala, and was very much interested in my plans. Naturally I also told him that I was going to Munich. "Then I have something for you that you probably don't know about," he said, and took an eight-page leaflet from among his papers. It was the statutes of the Johann-Albert-Widmanstetter-Gesellschaft zur Erforschung der Kabbala e.V. [Johann Albert Widmanstetter Society for Kabbala Research, Inc.] with headquarters in Munich, and there was also a membership form dated November 5, 1918. That was certainly cause for surprise. Paragraph 2 of the bylaws—and I have Buber's gift, which may be the only extant copy, before me—read as follows: "The purpose of the Society is the promotion of research on the Kabbala and its literary documents which have long been neglected due to accidental nonscholarly circumstances and under the influence of prejudices." Nor was that all: the chairman and vice chairman of the projected board of directors were none other than my two future thesis directors, Fritz Hommel and Clemens Bäumker, who had never breathed a word about this newly founded society to me!

Buber filled me in on the background. The Widmanstetter Society, he said, owed its existence to Dr. Robert Eisler, its "secretary" and actually its only active member. Stripling that I was, that name meant nothing to me, but Buber enlightened me. Eisler, the son of a Viennese millionaire, was an incredibly gifted man in his middle thirties, as agile as he was ambitious, and a person of very comprehensive scholarly interests as well as considerable writing ability. Buber said that he had published a highly interesting two-volume work with the attractive title *Weltenmantel und Himmelszelt* [Cosmic Cloak and Heavenly Canopy], which stamped him as an original and hypothesis-happy historian of religion, but which had been received by the experts in the field with great reservations. Eisler had also performed the unique feat of receiving two doctorates from the same school at the University of Vienna—one as a very young man in philosophy and one years later in art history—since it had occurred to no one that these two Eislers could be one and the same person. He had had himself baptized out of love for the daughter of a well-known Austrian painter, but despite this, his various attempts to obtain *Habilitation** had been blocked by distrust on the part of the departments involved. The Gentiles were made uneasy by his markedly Jewish appearance, and the Jews by his apostasy. Buber described him as the person who had had the idea of founding a society for Kabbala research; through correspondence and personal visits he had persuaded ten scholars well known at the time, including Buber, to lend their names as committee members supporting the aims of the Society

*A postdoctoral research project required for a teaching appointment at German and Austrian universities. —Trans.

(which, after all, made a lot of sense). Eisler had called on Buber early in 1918 (not long after my own visit to him) and had shown him the written consent of the above-mentioned professors (among them the son of Heinrich Graetz, who was a professor of physics in Munich). Eisler had submitted an essay to *Der Jude* in which he outlined the importance of this research for the history of religion in general and the understanding of Judaism in particular. Buber showed me the proofsheets of this essay (which are still in my possession). He said he had pointed out to Eisler that while he did print essays by Jews as well as non-Jews in the periodical, which was subtitled *Monatsschrift für lebendiges Judentum* [Monthly for Living Judaism], he could not very well include contributions by converted Jews, no matter what their motives for baptism might have been. Eisler had replied that he had long since decided to return to Judaism and was just about to take this step under the aegis of the Jewish Community Council in Munich. "I told him: 'Dr. Eisler, I shall have your article set in type, but I cannot publish it in *Der Jude* until you notify me that you have accomplished your reconversion.' " Since then, Buber said, he had heard nothing further from Eisler, though he had received the leaflet with the statutes which was graced by his own name. A year and a half having passed, he assumed that Eisler had retained his former status, and therefore he was making me a present of the article, which was not going to appear but might be of interest to me. At any rate, he suggested that I have a look at Dr. Eisler, who was living at Feldafing on Lake Starnberg.

I took Buber's advice, immediately obtained a copy of *Weltenmantel und Himmelszelt,* and was inspired by it to add to the catalogue of the "University of Muri" (as founded by Benjamin and myself) a course by "Professor Robert Eisler" on "*Damenmantel und Badezelt in religions-*

geschichtlicher Beleuchtung" [Ladies' Coats and Beach
Cabanas in the Light of the History of Religion]. And
now one of the most bizarre encounters of my life took
place. Eisler invited me to visit him in his little villa on
Lake Starnberg, which dated from his days as a millionaire's son. (During the inflationary period he, like almost
everyone else, lost everything except that house and
lived on "paying guests" from England.) For a few minutes
I was taken into a library crammed to the ceiling with the
most scholarly works about everything under the sun. My
attention was attracted by ten quarto volumes bound in
green morocco and bearing the inscription *Erotica et
Curiosa*. Without a moment's hesitation I pulled out one
of the volumes: it was just a dummy for cognac glasses
and bottles behind it.

Eisler received me with open arms. After all, I was,
so to speak, the heaven-sent angel who would breathe
kabbalistic life into his paper society. (Johann Albert
Widmanstetter, from whom the Society had taken its
name, died in 1557. Widmanstetter spent many years in
various missions in Italy, and his collection formed the
nucleus of the Hebrew manuscripts in Munich, including
the kabbalistic ones, with which I was going to spend the
next two years.) What better, then, could have crossed
Eisler's path than I? He told me about his own research in
the field, especially his "discovery" of the true author of
the Book of Yetzirah (the oldest brief Hebrew specu-
lative text, which probably goes back to Talmudic times
and which the kabbalists have appropriated as their basic
text). The substance of that research was so frivolous that
it only drew a skeptical shudder from me, since I was now
subjecting myself to serious philological discipline.

Eisler's eloquence was as fantastic as his education:
both were impressive but not quite serious. I, at any rate,
had never before seen such a brilliant, captivating, and

yet suspiciously glittering scholarly phenomenon. He displayed no rancor when he was challenged, and this trait made him particularly likable. But I was bound to detect before long the regrettable great gaps in his Hebrew. "I suppose you think I am a *nebbich* [pitiful] philologist," he once said, without even being offended. His imaginative deductions surmounted all hurdles of historical criticism. It could truly not be said of him that he lacked ideas, and utterly captivating ones at that; these ideas were in such diverse fields as the protosemitic inscriptions on the Sinai Peninsula, the Greek mysteries, the origin of the gypsies, the history of money, the origin of Christianity, and many other subjects which had one thing in common: they were all rich in unsolved problems which left the amplest scope to the combinatory mind. Anyone who heard his lectures was overwhelmed by his rhetorical gifts. If one read his writings, one was rendered speechless by the wealth of quotations and the references to the most unimaginable and most remote sources. I have never seen a comparable juggler of scholarship. His opponents (and he did not have very many defenders, although four or five of these were very influential) said of him with a slightly veiled anti-Semitic dig that he was a speculator who had strayed onto the field of scholarship. In short, he was unique in his way. But no publisher who had ever printed a book of his would have any further dealings with him, for in the course of reading proofs he would rewrite the book and make it at least twice as long, so that every publication project ended in a row.

Through Eisler I first learned about the circle that was forming in Hamburg around Aby Warburg and his library in the field of cultural history. In the early twenties Eisler gave a lecture there that was received with great enthusiasm, and which when published amounted to four hundred pages in small print. What Eisler told me about

Warburg and this circle was bound to arouse my lively interest in the new perspectives which were being opened
up there and which were to have such momentous conse-
quences. My own studies aroused great interest there from
1926 on, and after two visits to Hamburg in 1927 and
1932 I established close scholarly contact and friendly
relations with a number of persons from this circle. For
about twenty-five years it consisted almost entirely of
Jews whose Jewish intensity ranged from moderate sympathies to the zero point and even below. I used to
define the three groups around the Warburg library, Max
Horkheimer's Institut für Sozialforschung [Institute for
Social Research], and the metaphysical magicians around
Oskar Goldberg as the three most remarkable "Jewish
sects" that German Jewry produced. Not all of them
liked to hear this.

In his dealings with me Eisler was completely Jewish.
His store of Jewish jokes and anecdotes was virtually
inexhaustible, and it was understandable that he was able
to pour out his Jewish heart, which he held back tightly
when dealing with non-Jews, freely to someone like me.
This is not the place to go into his later scholarly and
personal fortunes, some of which were adventurous
enough, but I was in touch with him until 1938, when he
was able to go to England after some terrible weeks in a
concentration camp. In 1946 I received, out of the blue
and "with cordial regards," a 250-page English manuscript about the definitive solution of the Palestine question for which he was seeking a publisher (he never found
one). For years Eisler had been very pro-Zionist and had
informed me in letters that he was going to bequeath his
library to the Hebrew University. He now made a truly
original proposal amid rather unrestrained anti-Zionist
outbursts (this was the period when Ernest Bevin governed in Whitehall and tried to liquidate Zionism). All

those Jews whom a committee consisting of three Angli-
can theologians and three strictly Orthodox rabbis did
not declare kosher enough to be allowed to remain in the
country as pious worshippers were to be given a choice:
Either they could return to their countries of origin or (if
they wanted a Jewish state) they could take possession of
the second district of Vienna (the Leopoldstadt) as well as
the entire city of Frankfurt am Main. These territories
were to be evacuated by the Germans and placed under
international guarantees as a Jewish state. After all, after
everything they had perpetrated the Germans had now
forfeited the right to complain if Frankfurt am Main, the
most famous of all Jewish communities in Germany,
would be taken away from them and declared a Jewish
state. Eisler proposed that the British fleet be used for the
transport. I sent him the manuscript back with a slip on
which I had written only "Enough."

However, my first two books, which were published in
Germany in 1923 and 1927, managed to appear as vol-
umes 1 and 2 in the series *Quellen und Forschungen zur
Geschichte der jüdischen Mystik, im Auftrag der Johann
Albert Widmanstetter-Gesellschaft herausgegeben von Robert
Eisler* [Sources and Studies in the History of Jewish
Mysticism. Edited for the Johann Albert Widmanstetter
Society by Robert Eisler]. These were the only signs of
life ever shown by this fictitious society.

One day Eisler said to me that he had told Gustav
Meyrink in Starnberg about my kabbalistic studies and
that Meyrink wanted to invite me over to have me explain
some passages in his own writings to him. Naturally this
seemed very strange to me. In those days Meyrink was a
famous writer who combined an extraordinary talent for
antibourgeois satire (*Des deutschen Spiessers Wunderhorn*
[The German Philistine's Magic Horn]) with a no less

pronounced talent for mystical charlatanism. The latter quality was reflected primarily in his short stories, some of them very impressive but not quite serious, the literary quality of which has been surpassed only by Jorge Luis Borges in our time. At that point Meyrink had also published two widely read mystical novels, *Der Golem* [The Golem] and *Das grüne Gesicht* [The Green Face]. I had read them both and had to shake my head over the pseudo-Kabbala presented there. Thus I went out to Starnberg in 1921 with a certain amount of curiosity and made the acquaintance of a man in whom deep-rooted mystical convictions and literarily exploited charlatanry were almost inextricably amalgamated. He showed me a few passages in his novels: "I did write this, but I don't know what it means. Perhaps you can explain it to me." That was not very difficult for someone who not only knew something about the Kabbala but also about its misuse or distortion in the occult or theosophic writings of Madame Blavatsky's circle. But it also opened my eyes to how an author could score points with pseudo-mysticism. I will give only one example here. In the profoundly mystical chapter "Fear" in *The Golem,* the hero experiences a kabbalistic vision: a figure appears whose chest is inscribed with strange luminous hieroglyphs. The figure asks the hero whether he can read them. "And when I . . . answered in the negative, he stretched the palms of his hands toward me and the inscription appeared on *my* chest in luminous letters, at first in the Latin alphabet, CHABRAT ZEREH AUR BOCHER, then gradually changing into symbols that were unknown to me." I explained to Meyrink that this must be simply a mystical name of a lodge retranslated into Hebrew, something like "Lodge of Aurora's Seed," though I could not say whether such a lodge had ever existed or was fictitious. Not until fifty years later did I find out that it was nothing but a retranslation of the title of the so-called Frankfurt Jewish lodge, famous in the history of free-masonry from the days of Napoleon, namely the "Loge Aurora zur aufgehenden Morgenröte" [Aurora Lodge of the Rising Dawn], as incorrectly transcribed by some ignoramus in an English book in Meyrink's library.

Later, when we were drinking coffee together, Meyrink—whose ordinary appearance (he looked like the lowliest petit bourgeois) contrasted with the fantastic stories he wrote—told me about some of his own experiences. For example, he claimed to have cured himself of *tabes dorsalis,* an invariably fatal malady, by means of magical practices. Suddenly, without preliminaries, he asked me: "Do you know where God dwells?" It was hardly possible to give a precise answer to such a question, unless one wanted to quote the famous Rabbi Mendel of Kozk: Wherever one lets him in. Meyrink gave me a penetrating look and said: "In the spinal cord." That was new to me, and thus I made my first acquaintance with the famous Yoga work *The Serpent Power* by Sir John Woodroffe, alias Richard Avalon. Meyrink probably owned the only copy existent in Germany at the time.

I visited Meyrink once or twice more and was forever in a state of astonishment. He had the idea of publishing fictional biographies of great occultists and mystagogues and asked me whether I would be willing to write such a book about Isaac Luria, the most famous of the not merely legendary kabbalists. He himself planned to write something of this nature about Eliphas Lévi. *There* was a person who certainly belonged in such a series. As is generally known, the number of writers who hid their good Jewish names behind pseudonyms has been legion. Alphonse Louis Constant constituted the rare, if not unique, case of an author who took the opposite path and disseminated his imaginative charlatanries under a

Hebrew pseudonym as a *grand kabbaliste,* by no means
without success. Meyrink's last book, *Der Engel vom west-
lichen Fenster* [The Angel from the Western Window],
was based on the same idea, describing in a profoundly
mystical novel the life of Dr. John Dee, a famous scholar
and occultist of Elizabethan times.

To Eisler I also owe my acquaintance with Emil Forrer,
whose star as a young genius in the study of the ancient
Orient, especially Hittitology, was beginning to rise in
Munich at that time. (Later it was to fade somewhat.) He
had just proved that Hittite was an Indo-European language. Forrer and his wife, both in their middle twenties,
came from the Freideutsche Jugend and had an open
mind on the subject of Zionism. They repeatedly invited
Escha and me to visit them, and I was astonished at
Forrer's robust capacity for work. It was a pleasure to
associate with this couple. When they moved to Berlin
in the middle of 1921, they passed on to us their apartment on Gabelsbergerstrasse opposite the Technische
Hochschule [Technical College]. Years later it was one
of the unfortunately numerous shocks that the Hitler
period brought to each of us that even Forrer weakened
somewhat in regard to Nazism. His wife, who did not join
him in this and separated from him, later visited her
Jewish friends in Israel a number of times.

In Munich I had a chance to get acquainted with incipient Nazism at the university from close up. The atmosphere in the city was unbearable; this is something that is
often disregarded today and presented in more muted
colors than it actually was. There was no disregarding the
huge, blood-red posters with their no less bloodthirsty
text, inviting people to attend Hitler's speeches: "Fellow
Germans are welcome; Jews will not be admitted." I was
little affected by this, for I had long since made my

decision to leave Germany. But it was frightening to
encounter the blindness of the Jews who refused to see
and acknowledge all that. This greatly encumbered my
relations with Munich Jews, for they became extremely
jumpy and angry when someone broached that subject.
Thus my association with Jews was limited to a small
circle of like-minded people. One of them was Dr.
August Scheler, a justice of the peace (Amtsrichter) and
for several years chairman of the Munich branch of the
Zionist organization. In those years the philosopher Max
Scheler, one of the most distinguished philosophical
minds of the time, was talked about by all those with an
interest in intellectual life. He did everything possible,
the devil only knew why, to reduce his Jewish origin to a
minimum. Everyone who had spoken with Scheler gave
you a different version that had come directly from the
horse's mouth: according to one version, his mother was
Jewish and his father a Protestant; according to another,
the father was of Protestant origin but had converted
to Judaism for his Jewish bride's sake; or the father
was a Jew but the mother from a Christian family. Judge
Scheler was the spitting image of his famous namesake,
though his appearance lacked the gleam of genius. I
asked him what there was to all these stories and whether
he knew anything about the matter. Dr. Scheler laughed
and said: "He is my cousin, and of course I knew his
parents very well. Both were good Jews from old Bavarian
Jewish families, and Scheler was given a good Jewish
education. We find his bogus genealogies amusing, patho-
logical as they are." But the legend spawned by the
philosopher is repeated to this day.

For the Sabbath noonday meal I was frequently invited
to the home of Dr. Eli Strauss, the Zionist vice president
of the Munich Jewish community. There the Sabbath

songs sung before grace, especially the twenty-third
Psalm, were set to melodies I particularly liked. Strauss
was the great-grandson of one of the virtually mythical
figures of German Jewry whose name and legend enjoyed the greatest popularity among South German Jews
down to my generation. That was Rabbi Seckel Wormser,
famed far and wide as "the Baal Shem of Michelstadt," a
small town in the Odenwald. Eli Strauss and his brother
Raphael still possessed several manuscripts and documents of this Baal Shem, whose miraculous deeds served
Ernst Bloch as the subject of several wonderful pages of
reflections in his book *Spuren* [Tracks]. Once, in April
1920, Strauss told me, "The other day Emil Hirsch, the
big dealer in secondhand books, called me up. He has a
copy of Eisenmenger's *Entdecktes Judentum* [Judaism
Unmasked], which he advertised in the *Börsenblatt des
deutschen Buchhandels* [German Book Trade Gazette].
He has already received an offer on a postcard from the
Deutschvölkischer Schutz- und Trutzbund [Protective
Alliance of German Nationalists]. The card was stamped
with a large swastika. This made him a bit queasy; after all,
he is a Jew and doesn't exactly want to sell this kind of
book to an anti-Semite. He's asked me whether I can
recommend a reliable Jewish buyer to him; he says he
doesn't want to make any money on the book. Would
that perhaps be something for you?" Of course this was
something for me, for the Eisenmenger, with its two
terribly fat quarto volumes from the year 1700, was by far
the most famous, the most scholarly, and at the same time
the most stupid major work of anti-Semitic literature.
With my means I did not have any prospect of acquiring
it. So I went straight from the Sabbath table to Hirsch
on Carolinenplatz and told him who I was. He said:
"You know, all I care about is that the book gets into

the right hands. I paid fifty marks for it." That was a sum I could raise with pleasure; at the time it was equivalent to a half dollar.

I finished my dissertation at the end of January 1922 and prepared for the oral examination. Hommel told me: "Mr. Scholem, don't open a book the last two weeks before your exam. Take a walk in the English Garden and do anything you enjoy doing, but forget about everything that concerns the exam. That will be more valuable than any cramming." There was a perceptive man! In mathematics, my minor subject, I was assigned to Ferdinand Lindemann, and this gave me a certain feeling of elation. This, after all, was the famous man who exactly forty years earlier had disposed of the problem of squaring the circle once and for all. A candidate had to present himself to the examiner and identify the special areas in which he was most knowledgeable. Lindemann was rector of the university and did very little teaching any more. He received me graciously and said: "I understand you have taken nine semesters of mathematics, so you should really know quite a lot." At the examination on March 3 he asked me for the fun of it whether I could expound on Charles Hermite's sequence of ideas in his demonstration of the transcendence of the number e. The joke was that Lindemann's own proof that π is a transcendent number was actually only an ingenious application and elaboration of Hermite's proof. On the other hand, Bäumker, who knew me well, asked me in the half-hour at his disposal whether I could expound on Hermann Lotze's theory of propositions and take a critical stand on it. This took up the entire half-hour. Hommel said: "Hebrew and Aramaic you know better than I do, so why should I examine you on these?" But Hommel was enamored of South Arabic inscriptions, so he presented

to me a brief Sabaic inscription and had me read a few
verses from the famous *Qasida* of Imru-al-Qays, which I
can recite to this day.

My two principal teachers, Hommel and Bäumker (the
latter wielded a great deal of influence in the School),
invited me to a meeting the following day and offered me
Habilitation at the University of Munich, along with the
prospect of a teaching appointment in Jewish studies,
provided that I presented an appropriate piece of research. As I have already mentioned, that would have
been a novelty at a German university. Though I did not
seriously consider the offer, I was able to use this prospect as a trump card in dealing with my father, completing
my studies and preparing for my projected emigration.

On the following day, which was his birthday, my
father became gravely ill. A telegram called me to Berlin,
and for a few days the doctors held out hardly any hope.
But my father did recover, though only very slowly, and
from that time on he had to be very careful of his health.
My two elder brothers, who had gone into business with
my father, assumed the main responsibility for it. When
my father was out of danger, I returned to Munich to ship
my books and other things to Berlin. From there I went
to Frankfurt for a few days; in the meantime, Agnon
had settled nearby. I had been in Frankfurt for three
days the previous year and had seen Franz Rosenzweig
there several times. Rudolf Hallo, a young man who, like
Rosenzweig, was from Kassel and had for some time been
deeply influenced by him, had been my fellow student in
Munich. From Hallo I learned much about Rosenzweig,
his development and turning to Judaism, and early in
1920 Hallo brought me a copy of Rosenzweig's recently
published main work *Der Stern der Erlösung* [The Star of
Redemption], undoubtedly one of the central creations

of Jewish religious thought in this century. Thus I started corresponding with Rosenzweig, who had in the meantime heard about me from various sources. At that time Rosenzweig still had his health and had started to study the Talmud with the famous rabbi Dr. Nobel in Frankfurt. Every encounter with him furnished evidence that he was a man of genius (I regard the abolition of this category, which is popular today, as altogether foolish and the "reasons" adduced for it as valueless) and also that he had equally marked dictatorial inclinations.

Our decisions took us in entirely different directions. He sought to reform (or perhaps I should say revolutionize) German Jewry from within. I, on the other hand, no longer had any hopes for the amalgam known as "Deutschjudentum," i.e., a Jewish community that considered itself German, and expected a renewal of Jewry only from its rebirth in Eretz Yisrael. Certainly we found each other of interest. Never before or since have I seen such an intense Jewish orientation as that displayed by this man, who was midway in age between Buber and me. What I did not know was that he regarded me as a nihilist. My second visit, which involved a long conversation one night about the very German Jewishness that I rejected, was the occasion for a complete break between us. I would never have broached this delicate topic, which stirred such emotions in us both, if I had known that Rosenzweig was then already in the first stages of his fatal disease, a lateral sclerosis. He had had an attack which had not yet been definitely diagnosed, but I was told that he was on the mend, and the only thing left was a certain difficulty in speaking. Thus I had one of the stormiest and most irreparable arguments of my youth. Three years later, however, Buber and Ernst Simon asked me to contribute to a portfolio of very short essays which was to be presented to Rosenzweig, who was then already paralyzed and unable to speak, on his fortieth birthday, and I did so. When I was in Frankfurt in August of 1927, Ernst Simon said to me: "Rosenzweig would be very pleased if you visited him." I went and told the terminally ill man about my work. He could move only one finger and with it directed a specially constructed needle over an alphabet board, while his wife translated his motions into sentences. It was a heartrending visit. Yet Rosenzweig produced very impressive work even in those years, participated in the Bible translation project inaugurated by Buber, and corresponded copiously with many.

IX

Berlin and Frankfurt Once Again (1922–1923)

UPON MY RETURN to Berlin I reported for my *Staatsexamen* in mathematics and was given an assignment involving the theory of Euler's planes. I also bought the Hebrew mathematical textbooks which were being used at the Gymnasium in Tel Aviv in order to familiarize myself with the mathematical terminology I would have to know as a teacher in Eretz Yisrael. My father, who had been impressed by my *summa cum laude* doctorate after all and who thought my teachers' offer of *Habilitation* would break me of my "youthful foolishness," had my book printed in our printshop whenever a typesetter had a free hour or two. In those days, at the height of the inflation, that was no small matter. It had long been impossible to have doctoral dissertations printed, because no one was able to raise the money. At any rate, *Das Buch Bahir* [The Book of Bahir] was ready in a year and appeared in Eisler's abovementioned series under the imprint of Drugulin, the house where all the expressionistic literature published by Kurt Wolff appeared in those days.

In the meantime I continued my studies in the field of
the Kabbala. To deepen my knowledge of Hebrew literature I spent countless hours, particularly at night, in the
library of Moses Marx, with whom I had become friends
after my return from Switzerland. This memorable man
was a partner in a textile firm on Spittelmarkt, but his
heart belonged to Hebrew typography and bibliography,
though he was hardly capable of understanding the contents of the books which he so lovingly tended and had so
wonderfully bound by Berlin's most outstanding crafts-
men. He was one of the many victims of the illusion—
caused by the inflation—that they were very rich, whereas
in reality they had nothing left. Marx was the brother-in-
law of Agnon, who had first introduced me to him in
September of 1919. He was a very sensitive and easily
vulnerable man who combined an intensive Jewish feeling
with more than a touch of Prussian personality. Having
abandoned Orthodoxy, he had espoused Zionism. Later I
met several other people of this type, but Marx was its
most pronounced representative. We would often travel
on the upper deck of a bus from the Spittelmarkt to the
Helmstedter Strasse at the Bayrischer Platz. On a number
of occasions I stayed there from 7:00 P.M. to 7:00 A.M.
and fascinatedly browsed through the several thousand
volumes of his library.

Among the books which Marx possessed was a complete copy of Knorr von Rosenroth's *Kabbala Denudata,*
the most important Latin work on the Kabbala, which
appeared between 1677 and 1684; its volumes, which
totaled twenty-five hundred pages, were beyond my
means. But once Marx came to call on me at Neue
Grünstrasse in order to view my kabbalistic collection in
the making. My mother, who commanded an expressive
vocabulary, said to me: *"Na, was wollt ihr euch denn
gegenseitig abbewundern?"* [Well, what are you going to

admire each other out of?] Marx did find an extremely rare little *cabbalisticum* which had appeared at Saloniki in 1546 and still had its wonderful original Turkish binding with leather tooling. I had bought it a short time previously on my visit to Frankfurt for one hundred marks (then a half-dollar). Marx asked me: "What do you want for it?" "Kabbalistic books I can't swap," I replied. "Tell me anyway," said he. "Good grief, if you insist, I shall make you an offer which you certainly won't accept. Give me your *Kabbala Denudata* for it." Marx winced and said nothing. But the next time I came to see him he suddenly blurted out angrily: "Go ahead and take the stuff. The *Kabbala Denudata* can always be had for money, but your old book isn't to be had for any amount." Thus I came into the possession of the valuable volumes, and it really was fifteen years before I was able to acquire the little Saloniki book again at an auction in Amsterdam.

With my brother Werner I had a variety of contacts again following my return from Berne. Right after the end of the war he had plunged into politics, at first still in the ranks of the USPD [Independent German Socialist Party]. On my way to Berlin I stopped off to visit him in Halle, where he was editing the local party newspaper. A discussion flared up on whether a man like himself could really appear as a representative of the proletariat (the Leuna Works near Halle were a stronghold of the USPD). I accompanied him to a rally at which he spoke and kept my eyes and ears open. My brother was not untalented as a demagogue. "Don't fool yourself," I told him, "they'll applaud your speech and probably they'll elect you a deputy at the next election [which was his ambition], but behind your back nothing will change." I heard one of the workers say to his colleagues: "The Jew [not "our comrade"] makes a nice speech."

When I came to Berlin in 1922, Werner was there again as a Communist deputy of the Prussian Diet, living in a rear building on elegant Klopstockstrasse. After the USPD's split he had, in October 1920, joined the KPD [German Communist Party] along with that small majority that had swallowed the Comintern's then-sensational "Twenty-one Conditions of Admission." That was the beginning of the sellout to Moscow which at that time was still veiled in Marxist jargon. Anyone who made a peep was kicked out. The representative of the Comintern living in Germany, often illegally and under an assumed name, determined the party line.

In those days my brother was one of the KDP's chief orators in Berlin. I could not bring myself to go there even once. Our discussions were quite stormy, but we remained friends nonetheless. Werner told me quite a bit about the behind-the-scenes activities of the leaders sent from Moscow; of these, Radek and Guralski in particular played a deadly role. Like so many believers of the time, my brother defended the "revolutionary necessities" (read: the terror that shrank from nothing), which had played a central role in the debates since the Halle convention at which the split was decided. To be sure, as was the custom, my brother, like Grigoryi Zinoviev himself in that notorious Halle speech, simply denied most facts, though he accepted the theory supplied along with them. In this he may have been acting in good faith; I have never been able to determine that. I found the whole thing completely indigestible. My brother soon became the youngest member of the Reichstag, and this placed him at the head of the Nazis' blacklist. At a very early date he became embroiled in the exceedingly vehement factional fights of the KPD, and this led to his expulsion from the party as early as November 1926. He remained a Communist, but outside the party, which was

falling prey to Stalinism. After seven years of prison
and concentration camp he was murdered at Buchenwald
in July 1940.

Between 1921 and 1923 I had many dealings, albeit
indirect ones, with the group around Oskar Goldberg. (A
few pages in my book on Walter Benjamin are devoted to
this subject.) I met some of Goldberg's adherents, though
they did not belong to the inner circle of true initiates.
One of these was Wolfgang Ollendorf, the younger
brother of our friend Käthe Becher. Among the friends
of my youth from Jung Juda was Karl Türkischer (whom
we called by his Hebrew name, Kohos), a gifted person
with varied interests and the son of a wealthy and pious
Jew from Galicia who was a financial pillar of Bleichrode's
little synagogue association. We no longer had close contact with each other, and I was not aware that Goldberg's
people had won him over in the meantime. He told them
about me and my kabbalistic studies. The Kabbala was
highly regarded by them—not so much because of the
religious and philosophical aspects that had prompted me
to study it, but on account of its magical implications,
about which Goldberg (the only one in the circle who
really knew Hebrew) had the most extravagant notions.
In the early fall of 1921, shortly after Benjamin and I
had visited Wechterswinkel and had heard the strangest
details about Goldberg from Leni Czapski's husband, a
Miss Dora Hiller (a cousin of Kurt Hiller) sent me word
that she wished to talk with me. She had really done her
homework, had read my essays and translations in *Der
Jude,* and paid me the greatest compliments, particularly
on my translation of *Halacha und Aggada,* an important
essay of Chaim Nachman Bialik, who may be called the
Jewish national poet. (I had made this translation at
Buber's suggestion.) She said: "What Bialik—and pre-

sumably also you, his translator—are seeking is true authority. Here in Berlin lives the bearer of such authority, and you ought to get in touch with him." "And who is he?" I asked. "Oskar Goldberg," she replied. Stung by this eulogy, I reacted in somewhat overwrought fashion: "Madam, I know who Oskar Goldberg is, and I am inclined to regard him as a representative of the devil in our generation." Now the fat really was in the fire. Miss Hiller, who looked rather imposing in those days, rose and declared that she was taking back everything she had said to me and considered our conversation as never having taken place. She swept out of the room, and later I learned that she had become Goldberg's wife.

In March 1922 I met Türkischer once again, and it turned out that he was about to fall under Goldberg's spell. He said he had heard that my attitude toward Goldberg was entirely negative, and he wanted to know why. I warned him against becoming involved with this man, who was finding it impossible to realize his dreams of magical dominance and therefore sought to make up for it through the subjugation and exploitation of human souls. But as far as I recall, I was preaching to deaf ears. Gustav Steinschneider, on the other hand, did not become too involved with the sect, and not at all with Goldberg personally, and so he found the philosophical lectures and discussions which they held and to which he sometimes went with Walter Benjamin interesting, amusing, and basically inconsequential.

While I was still in Munich, brief writings of this group began to appear. Their authors, particularly Erich Unger, Ernst Fraenkel, and Joachim Caspary, betrayed a high degree of intelligence. In 1922 Unger published a metaphysical diatribe against Zionism with the nice title *Die staatslose Gründung eines jüdischen Volkes* [The Stateless Founding of a Jewish People], which was really quite something. It censured empirical Zionism, which the author rejected, for being deficient in "metaphysics," but what was meant was not so much metaphysics as magical power (and not just metaphorically) which, according to Goldberg's doctrine, ought to be possessed by metaphysically charged "biological entities." Instead of learning how to work magic properly, the Zionists—according to the author—were wasting their energies on building villages, settlements, and similar nonsense that could not promote the "magical faculty" of the Jews which needed to be renewed. All this was not so clearly expressed in the elegant language in which the lecture was draped, but intelligent readers were bound to notice that such was indeed the salient point of this remarkable essay. Later, in Goldberg's own writings, it was given drastic expression with all the requisite bluntness and appropriate invectives.

Strangely enough, Buber knew nothing about the activities of these new magico-metaphysicians. But when I told him about them on one of his visits to Munich, he said: "Oh, that actually reminds me of an incident involving Unger and Goldberg." During the war, in January 1916, a man named Herr Unger had shown up in Heppenheim to discuss an urgent matter with him. He had explained to Buber how important it was to end the war, and for that there was really only one means, namely to establish contact with higher powers that guided humanity and to induce them to act. These forces were the Mahatmas in distant Tibet, the famous sages of the Himalayan "White Lodge" invented by Madame Blavatsky. There was one person who could establish such a contact, and it was necessary to get him out of Germany so he could travel to India via Switzerland. Buber told me he had been utterly astonished and had asked Unger what function he could or should have in this. To Buber's even greater astonishment, Unger said that Buber was reputed to have excellent connections in the Foreign Office and thus could use his good offices to procure an exit permit for Dr. Goldberg. "Those people really seemed to believe that I had some sort of connection with the Foreign Office," said Buber; but he had had to disillusion them on that score. As proof of the supernormal abilities of Goldberg, whom Buber had never heard of, Unger produced Goldberg's pamphlet *Die fünf Bücher Mosis, ein Zahlengebäude* [The Pentateuch, an Edifice of Numbers] in which Goldberg—so he said—had proved by means of numerological calculations that the Torah must have been written by a superhuman intellect, let us say an Elohim. Years later I learned from Ernst David, who had belonged to the inner circle of the sect and had financed Goldberg's main work, *Die Wirklichkeit der Hebräer* [The Reality of the Hebrews], but had then "defected" to the Zionists, that his mentor had for a long time been among the adherents of Madame Blavatsky.

During my sojourns in Berlin between 1919 and 1923 I established contact with several young scholars, somewhat older than I, who were employed as researchers by an organization working toward the (never accomplished) foundation of an academy for the science of Judaism. This was an important beginning, for here it was not a matter of training rabbis and thus did not involve a theological commitment to some ideology or party within Judaism. Rather, the point was to establish a pure research center at which the religious, the irreligious, and atheists who cared about a knowledge of Judaism could work side by side in peace and quiet. Some were Zionists, some were not, but most of them were highly gifted researchers whose names and achievements still live on in the Science of Judaism, such as Fritz Yitzhak Baer, Hartwig David Baneth, Leo Strauss, Selma Stern, and Chanoch Albeck.

In particular, I quickly established amicable relations
with Baer, possibly the most outstanding and most profound historian of my generation, and with Baneth, a
first-rate Arabist. Baneth told me in the summer of 1922
that Professor Philip Bloch, the former rabbi of Poznán
and one of the last survivors among the better-known
pupils of Heinrich Graetz, had moved to Berlin and had
donated his substantial library (which Baneth was then
helping to catalogue) to the Akademieverein [academy
association]. He suggested that I visit Bloch, who at age
eighty-two was still very spry and was domiciled together
with his library. In the generation preceding mine, Bloch
had been *the* authority on the Kabbala, though an authority in Graetz's spirit. He had published an outline of
this field as well as a few specialized essays. Beyond that,
he was the only Jewish scholar in Germany who had
assembled a rich collection of kabbalistic works and
manuscripts. Bloch gave me a very friendly reception—as
a young colleague, so to speak. "After all, we are both
meshugga," he said. He showed me his kabbalistic collection, and I admired the manuscripts. In my enthusiasm I
said, quite naively: "How wonderful, Herr Professor, that
you have studied all this!" Whereupon the old gentleman
replied: "What, am I supposed to *read* this rubbish, too?"
That was a great moment in my life.

In those years the Zionists constituted a small but very
articulate minority in Germany. Of the Jewish population
of about 600,000, 20,000 participated in the election of
delegates to the convention of the German Zionist Association in 1920. Considering the voting age, this figure
bespoke a marked increase in the influence of this movement since the prewar years. The overwhelming majority
of the Zionists had a middle-class orientation. My sympathies lay with the radical circles which represented the

social ideal of the incipient kibbutz movement. When I still had friendly relations with the red publisher Klaus Wagenbach, he wrote me in a letter of about twelve years ago: "I've been reading some of your early essays. You were some *Radikalinski* in those days, hee hee!" As I have already mentioned, the anarchistic element in some groups in Israel, and by no means unimportant ones, came very close to my own position of that time. In 1921, when I read a journal article by a leader of these groups (he later became one of the most influential would-be Stalinists who molted in strictly Marxist fashion), his definition of the Zionist social ideal as "the free banding together of anarchistic associations" certainly struck a responsive chord in me. Beyond this it is safe to say that the overwhelming majority of those who went to Eretz Yisrael from Germany in the early twenties were motivated by moral rather than political considerations. It was a decision against what was perceived as a helter-skelter, dishonest and undignified game of hide-and-seek. It was a decision in favor of a new beginning which appeared clear-cut to us at the time—a new beginning which, whether it was motivated by religious or secularistic considerations, had more to do with social ethics than with politics, strange though that may seem today. We were as yet not fully aware of the dialectics that I have already mentioned. In those days we did not know, of course, that Hitler was going to come, but we did know that, in view of the task of a radical renewal of Judaism and Jewish society, Germany was a vacuum in which we would choke. This is what drove people like myself and my friends to Zionism.

Before I took that step there were a few interludes. In Berlin there was a Jüdische Volkshochschule [Jewish Adult Education Program], and it invited me in winter

1922 to give a course entitled "History of Jewish Mysticism"—a course that was astonishingly well attended. It was my first attempt to present myself as a teacher in this field. Today I can only shudder when I think back to these extremely immature lectures. Among my students were some unusual seekers, like one of Berlin's best-known violin makers and the later abbot of a Buddhist monastery and propaganda center in Ceylon who thirty-five years later began to send me a long series of English-language Buddhist texts and analyses.

Entirely different in nature was my last journalistic activity, an activity that was far removed from my field of study. The Jewish hiking club Blau-Weiss, against which I had polemicized five or six years previously, had in those days been strongly influenced by parallel developments in the German youth movement and had shifted to a position which can even today only be described as semi-fascist. The association gave itself a "law" which, if I may quote myself, was proclaimed in the vicinity of a Bavarian village "amid the Sinai-like thunder of four-hundred-year-old mercenaries' songs." For months not a word about these and related events was printed in the *Jüdische Rundschau* [Jewish Review], the journal of German Zionism which was already edited by Robert Weltsch, with whom I became good friends later. I wrote an explosive denunciation of this development, and it was submitted to the *Jüdische Rundschau* as a declaration signed by fifteen members of the *halutz* movement. Weltsch categorically refused to print it, possibly because the article excoriated the cowardice with which his journal had kept silent about all these goings-on. We demanded a ruling from the chairman of the Zionist Organization. My friend Heller and I presented our demand to Felix Rosenblüth, a serene man who later became the first Minister of Justice in the State of Israel, and Weltsch explained why he did not want to accede to it. Rosenblüth said nothing for two minutes and then decided that our declaration would be published, but in a new department headed *"Sprechsaal* [Open Forum]—The editors are not responsible for the views expressed." The appearance of our declaration created a certain stir; polemical tempers rose high, and since my authorship was readily recognizable by the passionate style in which I then wrote (and wrote for a long time in Hebrew polemics as well), I was treated to several rather unflattering harangues.

It was this polemic that initiated the friendship between Ernst Simon and me. We met at the end of December 1922 and liked each other almost immediately. Simon came from an even more de-Judaized home than I, and the road he had taken (and which had made him the favorite pupil of the distinguished Rabbi Nobel of Frankfurt) was not unlike mine, though it had been determined by altogether different factors, namely his experiences in the German army during the war. In those years Simon not only looked wonderful, he was also incredibly quick-witted, clever, and a brilliant speaker who took an equally brilliant doctor's degree under Oncken with a book about Ranke and Hegel. Without being really Orthodox, he had decided to live in accordance with Jewish law. He also told me about the circle that was forming around the Freies Jüdisches Lehrhaus [Free House of Study] that had been founded by Franz Rosenzweig and about Rosenzweig's progressive incurable malady. As I was also eager to see the kabbalistic manuscripts in the Frankfurt municipal library, these conversations led me to tell Simon that I was prepared to go to Frankfurt for a few months before emigrating to Eretz Yisrael. I was not going to give any lectures at the Freies Jüdisches Lehrhaus, but I would read some texts with him and a few others. In Frankfurt the atmosphere was lively and there were quite a few people who were seeking access to Jewish matters and with whom one could talk. These were fruitful months in my life.

A great deal has been written about the Lehrhaus. When Rosenzweig was incapacitated by his illness, his pupil and my Munich fellow student Rudolf Hallo took over its direction. The true star of the Lehrhaus was not Martin Buber to the extent one might expect, no matter how crowded his courses were at first, but Rosenzweig's great new discovery, the chemist Eduard Strauss. His equal was hardly to be found in Jewish circles but only among Christian revival movements. His crowded Bible lessons were speeches of an "awakened one" who spoke out of the spirit. If one may be permitted to use the language of Christian sects, they were pneumatic exegeses, and to this day I do not know whether anyone took them down, for he himself spoke quite spontaneously. His listeners were spellbound, as though they were held by a magic circle; anyone who was not susceptible to this kind of talk stopped coming, and this is what happened with me. Strauss had no prior Jewish background, and without being tied to Jewish tradition he nevertheless constituted a pure case of a Jewish pietist. Judaism as he saw it was a spiritual church, and it was precisely this aspect which I had not been able to stomach in his then widely read pamphlet against Zionism and which drove me away from this "conventicle Judaism" when it was served up to me personally. My courses were something like the exact opposite of his style. I read important texts in the precisely interpreted original with a limited group of students who already had some knowledge of Hebrew. These were mystical, apocalyptic, and narrative sources—the kind most likely to inspire pneumatic exegeses. Every morning from eight to nine, before the doctor at whose place we were studying began his consultation hours, I read the

Zohar's explication of the Book of Ruth. Among my
students were such interesting men as Erich Fromm,
Ernst Simon, and Nahum Glatzer. With a few other
students I read the biblical Book of Daniel, the first
apocalypse of Jewish literature, and a few stories by
Agnon. This gave much pleasure to my pupils and to
Agnon himself, for in those days he was not yet used to
having his works read in schools.

I spent many hours in the municipal library at the
Schöne Aussicht which guarded within its walls the most
important Hebrew collection in Germany—an incom-
parable treasure which during the Second World War
was burned along with the major part of the entire library.
The head of that section, Professor Aron Freimann, who
administered the collection he had for the most part
assembled, seemed to be a character right out of an
Anatole France novel. He was like a brother of the figure
whom France described at the beginning of *La Révolte des
anges* [The Revolt of the Angels]. Anyone who was in his
good graces (and I had the rare good fortune to be) got to
see great rarities and the most abstruse curiosa. If you did
not belong to those happy few, your life was no bed of
roses, for the card catalogue of the Hebrew collection
stood not in the catalogue room that was accessible to all,
but in Freimann's room. Every order slip passed through
his hands, and when it did not concern a book of the
garden variety, *he* decided whether the book was available
for circulation. Sometimes this led to rather unpleasant
scenes. For book lovers like Agnon and me, to be sure, he
had an open heart. But even I was not admitted to the
many hundreds of manuscripts still waiting to be catalogued which he had added to the catalogued basic stock
over a period of twenty-five years. Instead he would
occasionally bring me something from the store of secret
treasures, with the words: "This will probably interest

you." He also had a large stock of curious anecdotes from the history of the *Wissenschaft vom Judentum,* not least concerning various Frankfurt scholars. From Freimann, who was himself strictly Orthodox, I heard a *mot* of Raphael Kirchheim, a staunch reformer of the mid-nineteenth century whom the pious feared like the devil because he could "learn" better than they: "There is nothing more enjoyable than a good cigar over a page of *gemara* [Talmud] on Sabbath afternoon."

Besides the Jewish Lehrhaus another remarkable institution created a stir among young academicians in those days. That was a sanatorium which the wags called "Torah-peutic." It was run in Heidelberg by the strictly Orthodox psychoanalyst Frieda Reichmann, a cousin of Moses Marx and Esther Agnon, and in it the Torah and therapy were cultivated on a Freudian foundation. Some of my best students and acquaintances from Zionist youth groups, such as Simon, Fromm, and Leo Löwenthal, visited the sanatorium on an outpatient basis. With the exception of one person they all had their Orthodox Judaism analyzed away. When I reencountered Erich Fromm, Frieda Reichmann's most famous analysand and my Zohar pupil, in Berlin four years later, he was an enthusiastic Trotskyite and pitied me for my petit-bourgeois parochialism.

At that time Agnon lived at Homburg vor der Höhe, a place that attracted him not only because of its scenic beauty but also, as he liked to claim, because of the old Hebrew books which had appeared there two hundred to two hundred and fifty years earlier. In point of fact, Homburg had become one of the great centers of Hebrew literature at that time. Thanks to the inflation, living in Germany was tremendously cheap for people who received payment for their work in foreign hard currency, and thus many of the most important Jewish writers, poets, and thinkers had congregated there—for example, Chaim Nachman Bialik, at that time the indisputably brightest star of Hebrew poetry and a true genius of conversation, as well as Achad Ha'am and Nathan Birnbaum. Around such men gathered some outstanding minds of Russian Jewry. Such an illustrious group could hardly have been found outside Russia or later in Israel. Agnon often came to Frankfurt, where the big dealers in secondhand Hebrew books were located, and with equal frequency I went out to Homburg on the streetcar line 24 which travels this route even today. Agnon introduced me to those men and women, and Bialik gave me, the only *yekeh* (as German Jews were called by eastern ones) in that circle, a very friendly reception. A German Jew who could speak Hebrew and read kabbalistic books—he had never encountered anything like that, and he maintained his friendly interest in me up to his death. Whenever I went to Tel Aviv for the weekend, I was welcome in his house on a Friday evening. Agnon frequently took me along on walks with Bialik. Their conversations were memorable and it paid to listen to them. The members of that circle spoke Hebrew almost exclusively. Agnon, who always pronounced my name in the Galician manner, used to say: "Schulem, don't forget to write down in your notebook what you heard." Well, I had open ears but no notebook, and I did not write anything down.

The Homburg center could not survive the stabilization of the mark for long. With one exception I met everyone in Israel again one or two years later. When I said goodbye to Ernst Simon, who came over five years later, we had a conversation about our future. He often quoted something I said then which he remembered as particularly characteristic. According to him, I said unsolemnly and in purest Berlinese: *"Sie werden die Einhaltung der Gebote predigen; ich werde Vokabeln lehren. Wollen mal sehen, wo mehr herauskommt"* [You are going to preach obedience to the commandments; I am going to teach vocabulary words. Let's see which will be more productive].

With a very knowledgeable, somewhat younger member of the Frankfurt circle I arranged a joint passage from Trieste for after I had put my affairs in Berlin in order. That was Fritz (Shlomo Dov) Goitein, the scion of a famous Moravian-Hungarian family of rabbis; I had stayed with him on my earlier visits to Frankfurt and got along with him very well. He had had an excellent Jewish education—his father had been a rural rabbi in a Lower Franconian district—and had just taken his doctorate under the direction of Josef Horovitz, a first-rate Arabist. Goitein was a rare blend, for he was a person with an artistic, even poetic, vein who was at the same time a scholar and a born schoolmaster. This was immediately recognized by Dr. Biram, the director of the Haifa secondary school (one of the most highly regarded pedagogical institutions in the country) when he came to Germany in the summer of 1922 in order to recruit qualified teachers for his school. He gave Goitein a firm contract for the fall of 1923, by which time he would have received his doctorate. Dr. Biram also interviewed me in Berlin as a candidate for a teaching position in mathematics; but, as one would probably say today, he and I were not on the same wavelength.

In those days it was by no means a simple matter to secure an immigration visa to Palestine. The British mandatory government, which operated in a very timid manner, gave the Zionist Organization a fixed annual number of "certificates," and on the basis of these the recipients received a visa from the British consul. Understandably enough, these certificates were given almost

exclusively to *halutzim* who were going to work in the
agricultural settlements. Therefore, in order to avoid
diminishing the number of such immigrants as far as
possible, quite a few people procured fictitious (or—
as in Goitein's case—genuine) offers of employment,
and with these they were able to receive a visa as a
specialist outside the quota. (There were also capitalist
visas for those with sufficient money and investment
possibilities, but people like us did not fall in that category.) Thus Hugo Bergmann, the director of the Jewish
National Library in Jerusalem (which was to serve simultaneously as the library of the projected, though not yet
existent, Hebrew University), gave me a fictitious appointment as head of the Hebrew section. This had been
arranged by Escha, who had gone over six months before
me as the equally fictitious fiancée of Abba Houshi, the
future mayor of Haifa. We had decided to get married in
Eretz Yisrael.

Hugo Bergmann had met us both in Berne in March of
1919, and somehow I had made an impression on him. I
was impressed not only by the fact that he was the only
well-known *yekeh* of the time who had published philosophical essays in Hebrew, but also by his personality. I
had not particularly liked his essays in *Der Jude* or his
writings in Buber's spirit. But I was surprised to find a
person totally devoid of pathos who was open to all
intellectual and socially constructive matters, a man who
inclined to a vision of Zionism that was closely akin to
mine. Thus I wrote him early in 1923 about my intention
of coming over; he sent me a very encouraging response,
and Escha did the rest.

In Berlin I informed my father that I planned to emi-
grate at the beginning of September; that was the end of
any illusions about my *Habilitation*. My father said only:
"My son, I assume you realize that you cannot expect any

financial support for your undertaking from me." I replied that I fully realized this. We did not discuss the subject further, but he sent me the shipping clerk from our printshop to help me pack my library, which already comprised two thousand volumes and was shipped on a freighter via Hamburg. For reasons never quite clear to me I had to send customs a typewritten list of my books, and I still have a copy of it.

Shortly before my departure, the latter part of August, Zalman Rubashov, who had spent most of the time between 1919 and 1923 shuttling between Palestine and Europe, came to Berlin once more, and I told him of my impending emigration. That was the occasion for my first meeting with Berl Katznelson, a man of extraordinary stature who played a highly influential, morally decisive role in the Zionist labor movement in Eretz Yisrael. It was the beginning of a friendship that ended only with his death in 1943, a few hours after a memorable evening he had spent at our home.

X

Jerusalem (1923–1925)

IN THE MIDDLE of September I met with Goitein in Trieste. At that time there were no boats that sailed directly to Palestine. The Lloyd Triestino sent its ships only as far as Alexandria, and like almost everyone else making the crossing in those days we went as steerage passengers. The weather was excellent. Those who did not wish to travel via El Arish and Gaza on the railroad that the British had built during the war took a small coastal steamer from Alexandria. This boat called at the various Levantine ports, including Jaffa, where Escha was waiting for me at the harbor. I was able to confirm the truth of the first sentence of Arthur Holitscher's book *Reise durch das jüdische Palästina* [Journey through Jewish Palestine, 1921], which we often chuckled over in those days: *"Die Klippen von Jaffa sind keine Metapher"* [The cliffs on Jaffa's shore are not a metaphor].

When I first arrived in Jerusalem, on September 30, I was put up at Bergmann's home. I soon had a momentous decision to make, for within a short time I was offered two positions. The head of the Hebrew school system in the Jerusalem Zionist Executive had quickly learned of my arrival through Bergmann—considering the small size of Jerusalem in those days, this was not surprising—and sent word that he wanted to see me. The mathematician of the teachers college, a Dr. Hermoni, had just left; Albert Einstein, who had met him on his visit to Eretz Yisrael, had procured him a scholarship for advanced studies in the matrix theory and for further work in this field. This theory had turned out to be crucial to the mathematical presentation of the theory of relativity, and its inaugurator lived in Vienna. Thus an immediate replacement was needed. Dr. Lurje wanted to know whether I had really studied mathematics, could present a diploma or the like, and would be able to teach mathematics in Hebrew. I could answer all these questions in the affirmative in good conscience. "I can offer you the job," he said, "if you can start in a week. You would be entitled to a salary of fifteen pounds a month, but of course we cannot pay you, because, as you know, the Zionist Executive has no money." Instead of payment, I, like all other teachers and officials, would receive a credit voucher for a consumer cooperative where I could get everything I needed. In those days salaries were paid seven months late—and it did not occur to anyone to go on strike. Everyone knew that the Zionists had no money, and that whatever they had they needed for settlement work. I promised to think it over.

At the same time Hugo Bergmann, who had certified the fictitious job for me, offered me a real position as librarian of the Hebrew section of the National Library. "You're just what we need," he told me. "You know everything about Hebrew books, are a disciplined person, and are knowledgeable in Jewish matters. I can offer you ten pounds a month, which of course we cannot pay you . . ." (etc.). In this connection one must remember that Bergmann, a classmate and old friend of Franz Kafka (whose picture stood on his piano), was also a great admirer of Rudolf Steiner (which was more than I could say about myself), and that my serious occupation with the Kabbala especially attracted him. He told me that I could start right away. The working hours were from 7:30 A.M. to 2:00 P.M., which would leave me time for my studies in kabbalistic literature. "I shall write the Zionist Executive that we're putting you on the payroll as librarian. The Executive never answers any mail, so everything will be all right."

I weighed the two proposals: teacher of mathematics or librarian for Hebrew literature? Escha and I wanted to get married, and she was earning six pounds a month—a modest living wage at that time. As a teacher I would have to correct papers in the afternoon as well, and who could say whether my pupils would not laugh at my Berlin-accented Hebrew? (The prevailing accent in the Hebrew then spoken in Jerusalem was Russian.) In the library I would be dealing with books all day, and almost everything about them interested me; then, too, I would have my afternoons and evenings free for the study of my texts. Thus I chose the worse-paid position, and this meant the end of my mathematics, although my numerous mathematical books sat on my shelves for a few more years. Hugo Bergmann wrote to the Zionist Executive, but— oh, miracle of miracles!—three days later a reply came: "Please fire Dr. Scholem immediately. Are you not aware that the Zionist Executive has no money to pay an additional librarian?" Bergmann showed me the letter. "Nu?" I said. He replied: "Then we'll write another letter." "And in the meantime?" "Oh, in the meantime we'll pay you out of the schnorring fund." The schnorring fund consisted of the cash in hard currency left as a memento by tourists from England, America, South Africa, and other countries after Bergmann had explained to them the situation of the National Library, which was to serve as the university library in the future, but had no acquisition budget. Thus I was one of the few people who received their salary in cash.

There were other signs and wonders in the Zionist Executive as well, though in the London headquarters rather than in Jerusalem. In about five months a letter came from Dr. Leo Kohn, Dr. Weizmann's secretary for university affairs, in which he gave Bergmann the good news that the Executive had decided to acquire the famous library of the still more famous (even world-famous) Islamist Professor Ignaz Goldziher (Budapest) for a future Arabic Institute of the university. The Zionist women of South Africa had undertaken to raise the funds for this purchase. Now they would need a librarian trained as an Arabist and wanted Bergmann to recommend one to them. Bergmann showed me the letter. "Wonderful," I said, "this is the ideal position for my friend Baneth, who meets all the requirements. He knows Hebrew and Arabic perfectly, is painstakingly accurate in everything, acquired his bibliographic techniques in the course of cataloguing Bloch's library, and is dying for the opportunity to come here. He has just been offered a position in Cincinnati, but this would be perfect for him." Bergmann wrote to London that he had a candidate, Dr. Baneth in Berlin. "Great," replied Leo Kohn, "I know Baneth. Why didn't we think of him in the first place? What salary do you think we should offer him? Would twenty-five pounds be adequate?" Bergmann was jubilant: "Now we've got them! In Jerusalem they don't have ten pounds for you, and the Londoners ask whether twenty-five pounds would be sufficient for Baneth! I shall give them a piece of my mind and inform them that Baneth and you must be given parity: fifteen pounds a month for each." In this way I came to be legalized.

Something more needs to be said about my Hebrew accent. My memory was extraordinarily good, but it was purely visual. Thus from the beginning I made hardly any mistakes in writing the languages that I learned, for I could visualize the words written in front of me. My acoustical memory, on the other hand, did not amount to much. Then, too, I saw little reason to exchange my Hebrew as shaped by the Berlin cadences for the Russian accent, which was obviously just as incorrect. If everyone had spoken with a Semitic accent, influenced by Arabic— as did, for example, the Oriental Jews—I would probably have made a greater effort in that direction. In Munich there was an associate professor named Karl Süssheim who was the only one in his department able to pronounce Arabic with the proper accent. When he read mystical texts of Ibn Arabi with us in a seminar, we strove to emulate him, though not very successfully. In any case, I was not nearly as bad as the director of the Zionist Land Settlement Department, the famous Dr. Arthur Ruppin, whose lack of linguistic ability was proverbial. When the president of the German Peace Society, General von Schönaich, visited Eretz Yisrael and happened to hear one of Ruppin's Hebrew speeches, he exclaimed enthusiastically: "Oh, he's from Magdeburg too!"

In 1924 I began to publish in Hebrew, and I edited the first three volumes of a quarterly for Hebrew bibliography that had been founded by six experts and was published by the library. Since then I have written a large part of my works in that language. In the early years this was not always easy. Even though I had had intensive instruction in Hebrew, it was still a long way to go to that free

association within Hebrew thought and the imagery of
the Hebrew sources which makes possible a fruitful and
effective expression in Hebrew. I would say that the
number of German Jews of my generation who traveled
this road with some success has remained below ten. But
I was fortunate.

The time when I came to Eretz Yisrael, the beginning
of the twenties, was a high point in the Zionist movement.
An impassioned generation had come to Eretz Yisrael
expecting great things from work in Palestine, and was
making intense efforts to found a Jewish society that
would have a productive life of its own. Those were
important and wonderful years, despite the shadows that
were beginning to appear. People lived in rather small
circles, for there were not yet very many people in the
country. When I came, there were fewer than a hundred
thousand Jews, and yet something like a great impetus
came from these young people who had made the Zionist
cause their own. These young people—and it should
never be forgotten that Zionism was essentially a youth
movement—possessed something naturally that so many
youth movements fifty years later not only lacked, to
their great detriment, but even looked on as though it
were a dirty word. That something was historical consciousness. I have already mentioned the dialectics concealed in this historical consciousness of the Zionists, a
consciousness which I shared with all my heart and all my
soul: the dialectics of continuity and revolt. But it would
not have occurred to any of us to deny the history of our
people when we had recognized or rediscovered it as a
people. That history was in our bones, whatever we were
striving for now. With our return to our own history we,
or at least most of us, wanted to change it, but we did not
want to deny it. Without this *religio,* this "tie to the past,"
the enterprise was and is hopeless, doomed to failure

from the start. But these were not the big questions at that time. They became more pressing fifteen years or so later: Were we a sect or a vanguard for the masses to come? Did the Jews want to take up and develop their history or not? What could their existence be like in the historical environment into which they came? How could their life be established on firm foundations with or without or in conflict with the Arabs? It was on questions such as these that opinions began to diverge when I came to Eretz Yisrael.

My friends went to the new kibbutzim in order to put into practice socialist lifestyles and methods of production. Other people remained in the cities as teachers, officials, and merchants. Some became real-estate speculators—an almost sure-fire business that was the subject of vehement disputes between land reformers and capitalists. There was strong communication between the various places. There also was enormous hospitality, and it was years before I became accustomed to staying in a hotel occasionally. Wherever you went, you found a place to sleep. Everyone visited everyone. There was a time when there was hardly a closed door in Jerusalem or Tel Aviv, even in the literal sense of the word. When you went out, you left the house open; hardly anyone locked his door. It did not occur to us that there might be a theft. There was, in fact, no stealing, but when we returned, someone was often lying in our bed—the friend of a friend, who had been given our address and wanted to spend the night.

Escha and I were married in November of 1923 and moved into two rooms in an Arab house whose walls, believe it or not, were 4 feet thick. You see, they consisted of two stone walls separated by a space of almost three feet which was filled with all sorts of materials—bricks and the like. This created an excellent insulation which kept the house cool in the summer and relatively warm in the winter. There was no running water, electricity, or telephone, and we received no bills for such things. The water came from a big cistern. In years of drought we filled them with a hundred donkey loads of water that we bought from an Arab. The house was located on the Abyssinian Road, which still looked exactly as it had during the Turkish period. It started at Meah She'arim and, winding around the Abyssinian church, ended at the "Street of the Prophets," a wide street which was even paved to some extent and was lined chiefly with hospitals, Christian institutions, and foreign consulates. Only beyond this large street did the new Jewish quarter begin. But our sandy path, which was inhabited almost entirely by Zionists well known then or later, was already something like a Zionist center. The real-estate agent was a Jew who had been baptized by the mission. Our house lay directly beyond the still intact wall which separated the ultra-Orthodox Meah She'arim ("hundred gates") quarter from the quarters of the not-so-pious. In fact, it originally had only four gates, facing the points of the compass, for it had been built in 1871 like a fortress in the midst of the rocky desert, half a mile outside the old city of Jerusalem. One could say that outside the walls of this Orthodox paradise, we lived almost allegorically. The National Library was at that time located two minutes up the street; two minutes down began the main thoroughfare of this quarter where the secondhand bookstores were clustered together. Their owners, thank God, knew little about the treasures they frequently guarded, having acquired them for little money from the widows of deceased immigrants. True, they were able to read religious books, but Hebrew bibliography was unknown there. If, as I have indicated, my place of work was up there, my playground was down here.

Thus the Jerusalem to which I came was as though heaven-sent. To be sure, it was quite remote (especially given the transportation system of the time) from the Jewish villages and new settlements where my friends were preparing for their own settlement (for which they later went to the Jordan valley), but it did have other attractions, quite apart from its holiness. After the years of the First World War it was saturated with old Hebrew books the way a sponge is saturated with water. Jerusalem has always been the destination of many Jews from all parts of the world; they came here—most of them with their books—to pray, to study, and to die. During the war years, particularly in 1916, there was a terrible famine and a great many people died. Their books remained, and great masses of them lay around in the Jewish quarter of the old city and in Meah She'arim. The walls of the houses in this district were plastered with proclamations, anathemas, and curses directed at the Zionists, all their schools, and other works of Satan. Whatever the Zionists undertook, like the opening of the Hebrew University on Mount Scopus, was certain to be greeted with a fresh maledictive proclamation. In fact, even Abraham Yitzhak Kook, the Chief Rabbi of the Holy Land and one of the great figures of the national movement of renewal, did not escape the curses and threats of the fanatics. Thus, this Meah She'arim was a rather dialectical paradise, as is presumably in the nature of paradises. We represented the snake that crawled over the walls of this paradise.

Many books were bought, but there was hardly a market for kabbalistic ones. To be sure, there remained the last kabbalists who had gathered around a venerable center of mystic tradition and meditative prayer that had existed in the old city of Jerusalem for almost two centuries. However, they recognized only a certain orientation as truly authentic and worthy of delving into in its writings. They had no use for anything in kabbalistic literature that did not correspond to this orientation, let alone for the works of Hasidic literature, a kind of popular Kabbala. Thus I was one of the few buyers on this market, and if I had had enough money I might have cornered it before other collectors began to afford me competition. At any rate, my growing collector's fever for kabbalistic literature of all kinds and species was able to develop powerfully, the only limitation being my meager purse. What a great day it was for me when one of the noblest rabbis of Meah She'arim, a man who disdained all fanaticism, sold his marvelous library in order to furnish his daughter a decent dowry. When I came from Germany, I brought along six hundred volumes in this field. Since then I have accumulated a total of more than seven thousand, and in my youthful folly I once even had printed a negative catalogue, consisting of those titles not owned by me. The title of this catalogue was a biblical quotation which in the original means "Go in peace" [Gen. 44:17] but could also be understood to mean "Come to Scholem." (In Hebrew a title with a dual meaning has always been prized.) I paid a certain price for my insistence on negotiating with the book dealers only in Hebrew. I did read Yiddish, and I have already told the story of my first publication in book form, the Yiddish memorial book *Yizkor*, but I never had the opportunity—and perhaps never sought one—to speak Yiddish. If I had spoken Yiddish with my bookdealers, as did my most successful competitors among the collectors (including Agnon), I would have been able to acquire the books much more cheaply. I paid for what may be called my Hebraistic fanaticism.

I worked in an institution called National and University Library, but except for one building—the Institute of Biochemistry for which Dr. Weizmann, himself a biochemist, had raised the funds and which was then under construction—the university was not yet in evidence. In Jerusalem there was a committee of a few notables who carried on fruitless discussions about the coming university and its professorships. For the rest, no one in the country believed that the project which had been decided upon as early as 1913 and for which a symbolic cornerstone had been laid in 1918 (before the war's end) would come to fruition in the foreseeable future. Nor was there any lack of skeptics and opponents. After all, in those days there was a sizable Jewish academic proletariat, and if the designation of "doctor" as a "Jewish forename" was very much in fashion at that time, this was by no means intended as flattery. Was the number of unemployed Jewish intellectuals to be augmented even further by opening an institution that would issue diplomas? Many people shuddered at such a prospect. Besides, as I have already said, the Zionists had no money, even though they liked to use the idea of a Hebrew University in Jerusalem as propaganda at meetings. But things took an unexpectedly favorable course.

In the fall of 1922 Dr. Judah Leon Magnes—or Judah Leibusch Magnes, as he persisted in signing his name after a tempestuous discussion pro and contra the establishment of a professorship in Yiddish—settled in Jerusalem with his family. Magnes was one of the outstanding figures of Jewish public life in the United States, and although he was only forty-five he already had an extremely varied and often dramatic career behind him. This is not the place to write in detail about this extraordinary man, whom I knew for twenty-five years. He was a personality of great charm and complexity: an American radical, a Zionist of the Achad Ha'am stripe, a rabbi who had turned from Reform Judaism to a more conservative lifestyle, and a man who was clearly a leader. In the First

World War he had parted company with Dr. Weizmann's political orientation and had become one of the main public advocates of the pacifists. Even after America's entry into the war he had continued to espouse his views with great courage, and later he had found himself so deep in the socialist camp that he was regarded as a Bolshevist in the United States. At only thirty years of age he had become the rabbi of the wealthiest Jewish congregation of New York, Temple Emanuel on Fifth Avenue, founded and maintained by the children and grandchildren of Jewish immigrants from Germany. After a few years Magnes had resigned his office with a sensational speech about the bankruptcy of the Jewish Reform movement. But some of the pillars of that congregation and of American Jewry in general still regarded Magnes as a man of character and moral stature whose word meant something to them. Though Magnes had at first probably envisioned working in the socialist labor movement within Zionism, he began to take an interest in the projected university. It evidently was he who interested Felix Warburg and his wife, both of whom had great respect for Magnes, in the idea of a Hebrew University when they visited Jewish Palestine, such as it was, in April 1924. At that time Warburg was one of the most influential men of American Jewry—an important banker from Hamburg and New York who, coming as he did from a pious family, kept an open mind for Jewish interests without being a Zionist. When he left the country he gave Magnes a sealed letter; he had not previously told him what was in it, but it contained a check for what was then a very considerable amount for the establishment of a Judaic Institute at the university. This started the ball rolling, for now some other good Jews did not want to be called pikers, and the dream began to assume concrete form. Late in 1924 the Institute of Jewish Studies

was opened; in April 1925 the Hebrew University itself
was inaugurated with great ceremony, and Magnes was
named its Chancellor—that is, the big boss.

Lord Balfour, the author of the Balfour Declaration, as
well as greats of the Zionist movement from Weizmann
and Rabbi Kook to Bialik and Achad Ha'am, sat on the
tribune of the amphitheater, which had been carved out
of the rock of Mount Scopus only a short time previously.
I was among the thousands who excitedly followed this
ceremony, and I can still picture the old, magnificent-
looking Lord Balfour standing before the setting sun and
delivering his eulogy of the Jewish people, its achievements in the past, and its hopes for the future.

In the meantime a specially created committee of well-
known Jewish scholars searched for men of learning who
could grace a Judaic institute that would be devoted to
research into all aspects of Judaism and its history. There
was as yet no thought of diplomas, God forbid. The
search was for researchers who were to devote themselves
wholeheartedly to these studies for their own sake and
not for the training of teachers, let alone rabbis. It was to
be an institution of pure research without any particular
orientation, in which scholars of all tendencies would
rethink all aspects of this field and cooperate with one
another in the spirit of such a task. The great Jewish
scholars of that generation were all highly sympathetic,
but none of them was willing to come to Jerusalem for
more than a semester or a year. Thus men of the younger
generation now also got an unprecedented chance to help
build the new institute, which would not be a rabbinical
seminary but a place of free scholarly inquiry.

They scoured the Jewish world, and Magnes's attention
was directed to me as well. Kabbala? What a peculiar
subject! But it was wonderfully suited for this institute,
which was more of an academy. It would never have

occurred to anyone to choose the Kabbala as a branch of study, but it did fit beautifully into the scheme as a pure object of research in which, according to the general consensus, almost everything still needed to be done. And the young man who had really delved into this field was already in Jerusalem and would not even have to be paid relocation expenses. But how could his full scholarly qualifications be ascertained? Of course, I had three advocates on the committee: Chaim Nachman Bialik, Martin Buber, and Aron Freimann, all of whom knew me. But Bialik was, after all, a poet; Buber's name was then not exactly considered the best recommendation by the great Jewish scholars, though one could not very well disregard him; and Freimann was an important bibliographer but neither a philosopher nor a historian of religion. Magnes wrote to two universally recognized authorities—not for Kabbala, where there were none, but for Jewish philosophy and Science of Judaism generally. One of these was Julius Guttmann, the head of the academy institute in Berlin which I have already mentioned; he warmly recommended me on the strength of my philosophical education and my previous work. The other one was Immanuel Löw in Szegedin, at that time one of the "grand old men" of the *Wissenschaft vom Judentum*. Löw was a scholar with an encyclopedic education and a specialist in botany in rabbinic literature. To this day he is widely known as the author of the five-volume work *Flora der Juden* [The Flora of the Jews], and I think I am the only one who ever laughed at this strange title. Löw wrote that I should definitely be appointed. He had read my book and found there two excellent pages on the bisexuality of the palm tree in kabbalistic literature. He added that the man who had written them could be relied upon. Thus began my academic career.

Index

Temple Israel

Minneapolis, Minnesota

In Honor of the Bat Mitzvah of
SUSANNA LYNN BLUMENTHAL
by
Dr. & Mrs. Malcolm N. Blumenthal

November 15, 1980